The End of Economic Man

Transaction Books by Peter F. Drucker

Adventures of a Bystander

The Age of Discontinuity

Concept of the Corporation

The Ecological Vision

The End of Economic Man

A Functioning Society

The Future of Industrial Man

Landmarks of Tomorrow

The New Realities

The New Society

The Pension Fund Revolution

The End of Economic Man

THE ORIGINS OF TOTALITARIANISM

Peter F. Drucker

WITH A NEW INTRODUCTION BY THE AUTHOR

Transaction Publishers
New Brunswick (U.S.A.) and London (U.K.)

Third printing 2009
New material this edition copyright © 1995 by Peter F. Drucker.
Originally published in 1939 by The John Day Company.

This book is printed on acid-free paper that meets the American National
Standard for Permanence of Paper for Printed Library Materials.

Library of Congress Catalog Number: 92-7063
ISBN: 978-1-56000-621-3
Printed in the United States of America

Library of Congress Cataloging-in-Publication Data

Drucker, Peter Ferdinand, 1909-
     The end of economic man: the origins of totalitarianism/Peter F. Drucker.
          p. cm.
     Originally published: New York: John Day Co., 1939. With new introd.
     ISBN 1-56000-621-8
          1. Europe—Politics and government—1918-1945. 2. Fascism.
     I. Title.

D443.D78   1992
320.94—dc20   92-7063

To Doris

CONTENTS

INTRODUCTION TO THE
TRANSACTION EDITION

The End of Economic Man was my first book, and at the time of its publication I was still an unknown young man. Yet the book received tremendous attention when it came out in the spring of 1939, and was an instant success. It was even more successful in Britain than in the United States. Winston Churchill, then still out of office, wrote the first review, and a glowing one. When, a year later, after Dunkirk and the fall of France, he became prime minister he gave the order to include *The End of Economic Man* in the book kit issued to every graduate of a British Officers' Candidate School. (It was, appropriately enough, packaged together with Lewis Carroll's *Alice in Wonderland* by somebody in the War Department with a sense of humor.)

Although this book was published more than fifty years ago, it was actually written even earlier. It was begun in 1933, a few weeks after Hitler had come to power. An early excerpt—the discussion of the role of anti-Semitism in the Nazi demonology and the reasons for its appeal—was published as a pamphlet by an Austrian Catholic and anti-Nazi publisher in 1935 or 1936. And it was finished between April 1937, when I first arrived in the United States from England, and the end of that year. It was the first book to try to explain the origins of totalitarianism—its subtitle. It has kept on selling. Indeed it has been reissued several times before this republication as a Transaction book, the last time in 1969 (the preface to that reissue is included in this volume). And lately the book has again gotten a fair amount of scholarly attention.

But for a long time during the nineteen-sixties—and indeed, well into the nineteen-seventies—the book was pointedly ignored by the scholarly community. One reason: it was not "politically correct" to use current jargon. It fitted neither of the two politically acceptable theses of the postwar period: the thesis that Nazism was a "German" phenomen to be explained by German history, German character, German specifics of one kind or another or the Marxist thesis of Nazism as the "last gasp of dying capitalism." This book, instead, treated Nazism—and totalitarianism altogether—as a *European* disease, with Nazi Germany the most extreme, most pathological manifestation and with Stalinism being neither much different nor much better. Anti-Semitism, for instance, appeared first as persecution and popular demagoguery in France, rather than in Germany, in the Dreyfus Affair of the eighteen-nineties. And it was the failure of Marxism—rather than that of capitalism—as a creed and as a savior, *The End of Economic Man* asserted, that led to the "despair of the masses" and made them easy prey to totalitarian demagoguery and demonology.

But there was a second reason why the book did not fit into the scholarly climate of the postwar period. It is the more important one, simply because the climate still persists. This book treats a major social phenomenon as a *social* phenomenon. This is still largely considered heresy (except by such fellow-heretics as the publishers of Transaction books and *Society* magazine). Major social phenomena are treated either as political and economic history, that is, in terms of battles, armies, treaties, politicians, elections, national-income statistics, and so on. (A good example for Germany and Nazism are the excellent books of the Stanford historian Gordon Craig, for example, his 1978 book *Germany: 1866-1945*.) Such developments are also explained in terms of "isms," that is, in terms of all-embracing philosophies. The prototype and exemplar of this approach for our theme is the 1951 book by Hannah Arendt *The Origins of Totalitarianism* which blames Hitler and Nazism on the systematic German philosophers of the early nineteenth century: Fichte, Schelling, or Hegel.

No matter how valid either approach, they are not adequate by themselves. The stool needs a third leg. Social phenomena need *social* analysis, an analysis of the strains, stresses, trends, shifts, and upheavals in society. This, I would maintain, is what sociology was meant to do, was indeed invented for in the early years of the last century. It is what the great men of sociology, a Max Weber (1864-1920) or a Vilfredo Pareto (1864-1923), did. It is what Joseph Schumpeter (1883-1950) did when he identified the "innovator" as the social force that turns economies upside down; the innovator does not behave economically, does not try to optimize, is not motivated by economic rationale—he is a social phenomenon. It is what this book tries to do.

"Society" is vague and impossible to define, argue my historian friends, my economist friends, my philosopher friends. They are absolutely right. But equally resistant to definition are history, economics, philosophy, nation, science, and poetry—indeed everything worthwhile thinking, talking, and writing about.

Yet all of us know what to do with these terms—"plus or minus 80%" as the statisticians would say—that is, adequate for operational purposes (despite everything the linguistic logicians say to the contrary). *The End of Economic Man* treats society as the environment of that very peculiar critter, the human being. History treats what happens on the surface, so to speak. "Isms"—that is philosophical systems—may be called the atmosphere. But society is the "ecology."

This book does not attempt to define "society." It tries to understand it. Whether it succeeds in this attempt readers must decide for themselves. But this book was the first attempt to understand the major *social* phenomenon of the first half of this century, that is, the rise of totalitarianism as a *social* event. It is still, half a century later, the only such attempt. This alone, I hope, makes it worthwhile reading.

PETER F. DRUCKER

Claremont, California
October 1994

PREFACE TO THE 1969 EDITION

When this book first came out, in 1939—thirty long years ago—it was shockingly unconventional and heretical. It was, of course, by no means alone in its uncompromising rejection of the totalitarian creeds, or even in its firm conviction that Nazism was pure evil sans qualification or extenuation. But the other books—and there were hundreds of them—all explained away Hitler in those years before World War II. They either came up with some pseudo-history of Nazism as a "manifestation of German national character," or they depicted Nazism (and Fascism) as the "dying gasp of capitalism," with Marxist socialism as the coming saviour. In this book, however, the "national-character" explanation is dismissed as intellectually shoddy; national character or national history may explain how a people does things, but not what things it does. This book rather diagnosed Nazism —and Fascism—as a pervasive sickness of the European body politic. And instead of proclaiming Marxism as the coming saviour, I asserted that the total failure of Marxism had been a main reason for the flight of Europe's masses into the fervency of totalitarian despair.

These views, and the conclusions to which they led,

were so heretical in the nineteen-thirties that I myself hesitated a long time before publishing them. The first draft of this book containing its main theses was actually done when Hitler was coming to power in 1933; I was, however, so perturbed by my own findings, inescapable though they seemed, that I decided to hold the manuscript until I could test its conclusions against actual events. But even after my predictions had been proven correct by the developments of the 'thirties, no publisher was willing for a long time to bring out the book. It was far too "extreme" in its conclusions: that Hitler's anti-Semitism would be propelled by its inner logic towards the "ultimate solution" of killing all Jews; that the huge armies of Western Europe would not offer effective resistance to the Germans; or that Stalin would end up signing a pact with Hitler.

Only after Munich, in the fall of 1938, did the late Richard J. Walsh, Sr., then head of John Day, the publishers, accept this book. He tried even then to make me tone down these "extreme" conclusions and imply them rather than come straight out with them. Yet Richard Walsh, who was both a publisher and a leading liberal journalist of the times, was singularly well-informed. He was also a courageous man who took quite a risk in publishing this book, and was, indeed, sharply attacked by "liberal" reviewers, most of whom in those days deluded themselves with dreams of Marxist utopia.

Six months after this book had first come out, in the spring of 1939, Stalin did, however, (as I had predicted) ally himself with Hitler. Another twelve or eighteen months later, in the bleak winter of 1940-41, after Dunkirk and the Fall of France, the British selected *The End of Economic Man* as the one political book to distribute to the young men preparing to be officers of the first nation that chose to fight the Nazi evil.

The word "alienation" was not in the political vocabulary of the nineteen-thirties and cannot be found in the pages of *The End of Economic Man*. Still, that Western man had become alienated from Western society and Western political creeds is a central thesis of this book. In some ways, *The End of Economic Man* anticipated by more than a decade the existentialism that came to dominate the European political mood in the late nineteen-forties and early nineteen-fifties. Two key chapters of the book are respectively entitled, "The Despair of the Masses," and "The Return of Demons," terms that, though quite familiar today, were rudely foreign to the political rhetoric of the 'thirties or indeed of any earlier period since the French Revolution. *The End of Economic Man* was also, as far as I know, the first political book which treated Kierkegaard as a modern thinker relevant to modern politics.* Yet, in sharp contrast to the massive literature on existentialism and alienation since World War II *The End of Economic Man* is a social and political rather than a philosophical, let alone a theological, book. Its first sentence reads: *"This is a political*

---

*Altogether he was so unknown then that the publisher's copy editor had trouble verifying the spelling of his name.

book." To be sure, it considers doctrines, philosophies, political creeds. But it treats them as data in a concrete analysis of political dynamics. Its theme is the rise of a power rather than the rise of a belief. It is not concerned much with the nature of man and indeed not even with the nature of society. It treats one specific historical event: the breakdown of the social and political structure of Europe which culminated in the rise of Nazi totalitarianism to mastery over Europe. Politics, society, economics, rather than spiritual agonies, form the plot of this book.

Yet, unlike every other book of this period, *The End of Economic Man* explained the tragedy of Europe as the result of a loss of political faith, as a result of the political alienation of the European masses. In particular, it traces the headlong rush into totalitarian despair to the disillusionment with the political creeds that had dominated the "Modern Age" which had begun three hundred years earlier. The last of these creeds had been Marxism. And the final, the ultimate, cause of the rise of totalitarianism was the total failure of Marxism to make sense out of political reality and social experience. As a result, the European masses were overwhelmed by a "return of the demons." Central to the Modern Age had been the belief that society could be made rational, could be ordered, controlled, understood. With the collapse of Marxism as a secular creed, society became again irrational, threatening, incomprehensible, menaced by sinister powers against which the individual had no defense. Unemployment and war were the specific "demons" which obsessed the society of the inter-war years. The secular creeds of Liberal Europe—and Marxism was their logical and ultimate formulation and their dead end—could neither banish nor control these forces. Nor could any existing economic or political theory explain them. Though human and social in origin and within society, they proved as irrational, as unmanageable, as senseless and capricious as had been the demonic forces of a hostile nature before which earlier men had grovelled in impotent despair.

Yet twentieth-century men could not return to the rationality of the religious faiths that had given spiritual certainty to their forebears.

The End of Economic Man was perhaps least fashionable for its time in its respect for religion and in the attention it paid to the Christian churches. Insofar as contemporary *political* analysis paid attention at all, it considered religion an outmoded relic and the churches ineffectual reactionaries. Stalin's famous outburst: "How many divisions has the Pope?", shocked only the way a four-letter word shocks in the Victorian drawing room; it said bluntly what most people knew very well but covered up by polite circumlocution. My book, however, has a chapter, "The Failure of the Christian Churches," which argues that the churches could have been expected to succeed, could have been expected to provide the new foundation. In this chapter, the Christian churches are seen as the one potential counterforce and the one available political sanctuary. The contemporaries, thirty years ago, still children of eighteenth-century Enlightenment and nineteenth-century Anti-Clericalism, tended to ignore the Christian dissenters—from Kierkegaard to the worker-priests of France—as isolated romantics, hopelessly out of touch with reality. *The End of Economic Man* was, to my knowledge, the first book that perceived them the way we tend to perceive them now, that is, as hard-headed realists addressing themselves to the true problems of modern society. This enabled the book to foreshadow both the emergence of Christian-Democratic parties that have been so prominent a feature of postwar Europe, and the "aggiornamento" of the Catholic Church under Pope John.

But *The End of Economic Man* also reached the conclusion that the churches could not, after all, furnish the basis for European society and European politics. They had to fail, though not for the reasons for which the contemporaries tended to ignore them. Religion could indeed offer an answer to the despair of the individual and to his existential agony. But it could not offer an answer to the despair of the masses. I am afraid that this conclusion still holds today. Western Man—indeed today Man altogether—is not ready to renounce this world. Indeed he still looks for secular salvation, if he expects salvation at all. And churches, especially Christian churches, can (and should) preach a "social gospel." But they cannot (and should not) substitute politics for Grace, and social science for Redemption. Religion, the critic of any so-

ciety, cannot accept any society or even any social program, without abandoning its true Kingdom, that of a
Soul alone with its God. Therein lies both the strength
of the churches as the conscience of society and their
incurable weakness as political and social forces in
society.

There was much talk of "revolution" in those years.
What was meant by the term was, however, a game of
musical chairs, that is, the replacement of the "capitalist
bosses" by the Marxist "Dictatorship of the Proletariat."
This book can claim to have been the first to realize that
this would simply be exchanging King Stork for King
Log, and that indeed the new rulers would be forced to
freeze the existing patterns of power and institutions. This
is commonplace today after Orwell's *1984*, Milovan
Djilas' *The New Class*, or the Russian invasion of Czechoslovakia in the fall of 1968. But it was quite new thirty
years ago when even the "anti-Communists" (indeed particularly the "anti-Communists") were absolutely sure
that communism would indeed revolutionize society
rather than replace one rulership group by another, an
infinitely more rigid and autocratic one.

One result of my findings that what was called "revolution" then—and is, of course, still called "revolution" in
Moscow today—was a power grab and very little else, was
the conclusion that the specific social and economic institutions of the system of production and distribution, that
was known as "capitalism," would survive and would,
in all likelihood, prove itself capable of economic performance. Marxism, however, because of its millennial

nature, I concluded, could not survive the first doubt in
its infallibility. When I reached this conclusion thirty
years ago, nothing was more "obvious" to anyone than
that the traditional economy could not possibly outlast
war. The actual experience we have had since would have
been unimaginable then: the resurgence of an economically "affluent" Europe and of an expanding world economy based on economic entrepreneurship organized in
privately owned and privately managed world-wide corporations.

But while I realized that what to the contemporaries
appeared as "inevitable revolution" was not likely to
happen, I also realized that the new totalitarianisms, especially Nazism in Germany, were indeed a genuine revolution, aiming at the overthrow of something much more
fundamental than economic organization: values, beliefs,
and basic morality. It was a revolution which replaced
hope by despair, reason by magic, and belief by the frenzied, bloodthirsty violence of the terror-stricken.

The End of Economic Man was meant to be a concrete
social and political analysis of a profound crisis. It was
not conceived as "history," and is not written as such.
But it also does not "report" events. It tries to understand
them. It might, therefore, be read today as a portrait,
perhaps a self-portrait, of the period and as a perception
of those nightmare years between the two world wars.
What comes through perhaps most strongly are the pervasive realities of these years which to us today, thirty
years later, are almost inconceivable.

The most surprising of these realities of 1939 to the

reader of 1969 will probably be that Europe was then the
stage of world affairs. This book was written by a man
living in the United States, at home there, and deeply
enmeshed in its politics and economics. Indeed by the
time this book came out, I was actually teaching American History and American Economics. I had also, by
that time, begun to develop a deep interest in Asia—in
Japan, above all, but also in India. (Indeed this interest
in Asia was indirectly responsible for the publication of
this book in 1939. For Richard Walsh, Sr., was not only
the head of the John Day Company and, as such, a publisher, but he was also the editor of *Asia* magazine; and
it was in the latter capacity that I first got to know him.)
And yet the book takes for granted that what happens in
Europe is what matters and decides. Franklin D. Roosevelt's America is, of course, mentioned many times in
The End of Economic Man. And it is clear, right from the
beginning, that its author hoped that America would
prove immune to the infection that was destroying Europe
and would overcome it in her own system and society.
But otherwise the United States is clearly relegated to the
rank of spectator. Similarly, colonial problems are mentioned only to be pushed aside. The fate of the world was
at stake in Europe and would be decided there.

Today such a view would be almost unthinkable. It is
precisely because General de Gaulle believed in such a
Europe-centered world that he smelled so strongly of
mothballs, even to his most fervent disciples. And yet even
General de Gaulle did not assume that Europe today *is*

the center. He only believed that it should be the center and that no other world center is right or even possible.

Thirty years ago, however, Europe *was* indeed the center. It was not totally insane for Hitler to believe that he could dominate the world by making himself master of Europe. Actually, Hitler was more realistic than any of the other European politicians of his time, Stalin included. He realized that his was the last opportunity for a European world empire and that the center of world politics was about to shift away from Europe. The others, including the non-Europeans, all shared de Gaulle's belief that Europe's dominance and centricity were ordained and part of the eternal order.

The second feature of the time portrayed in this book —and hard to imagine today—is the star role of Marxism in the constellation of movements, philosophies and emotions. I myself have never been attracted to any form of Marxism. And this book proclaimed—and tried to prove —that Marxism had failed and had indeed lost all relevance for the industrially developed countries. Yet Marxism—to paraphrase the title of a book that appeared almost twenty years after *The End of Economic Man*— was "the God that failed." The creative era of Marxism had come to an end with World War I. In the decades before it had been the inspiration to all creative thinking in politics, society, and economics on the European scene. Even the anti-Marxists of those days had to define themselves in terms of their position towards Marx; and "non-Marxists" did not exist in Europe during the decades before World War I. After the failure of the Socialist International to avert or to settle World War I, followed by the failure of communism to come to power in any single developed European country despite the collapse and chaos which 1918 left behind on the Continent among victors and vanquished alike, Marxism rapidly lost its vigor and became a ritualized but meaningless chant.

The intellectual elite which, before 1914, had been mesmerized by Marxism, deserted it almost entirely after 1918 and flocked to new leaders and to new thoughts. Max Weber in Germany, the Neo-Thomists in France, or Freud in Austria—to mention only the most prominent of the new intellectual lights—were not "anti-Marxist." They simply considered Marx irrelevant, by and large. And Marxism itself, which had thrown up a galaxy of thinkers and of political leaders before 1914, did not after World War I produce one single figure, even of the second rank.

But while Marxism rapidly lost credence and creativity for the intellectual elite, it became popularized. The vocabulary everywhere became Marxist, very much the way the American popular vocabulary suddenly became psychoanalytical in the mid-fifties. Marxism, no longer the solid gold of the "highbrows," became the small change of the "middlebrows." Marxism itself could no longer organize effectively for gaining power or even for gaining adherents, whether by the ballot box or by revolution. But demagogues could, with impunity, use Marxist rhetoric and could, as Mussolini did, cover up their intellectual nakedness by an "anti-Marxism" itself com-

posed of Marxist tatters. This happened even in the United
States. During its creative period, Marxism had not had
any impact on America. There is not one American
thinker or American politician, not even of the second
rank, who was influenced by Marxism to the slightest degree. But in its decay in the late 'thirties and early 'forties,
Marxism suddenly began to supply the rhetoric of the
pseudo-intellectuals and to serve them, for a decade, as
a substitute for thinking and analysis.

In other words, Marxism, "the God that failed," dominated the European political scene more pervasively after
it had become a corpse than it had done in its prime as a
secular religion. And this comes out clearly in *The End
of Economic Man*, where the failure of Marxism rather
than its threat or its promise is shown to be the central
factor in the rise of totalitarianism and a main reason of
the flight of the masses into totalitarian despair.

The last reality of the 'thirties which *The End of Economic Man* clearly conveys is the total absence of leadership. The political stage was full of characters. Never
before, it seems, had there been so many politicians, working so frenziedly. Quite a few of these politicians were
decent men, some even very able ones. But excepting the
twin Princes of Darkness, Hitler and Stalin, they were all
pathetically small men; even mediocrities were conspicuous by their absence. The very villains, a Papen, a Laval,
a Quisling, were pygmies whose foul treason was largely
boneheaded miscalculation.

"But," today's reader will protest, "there was Church-

ill." To be sure, Churchill's emergence as the leader in
Europe's fight against the evil forces of totalitarianism,
was the crucial event. It was, to use a Churchillian phrase,
"the hinge of fate." Today's reader is indeed likely to
underrate Churchill's importance. Until Churchill took
over as leader of free peoples everywhere, after Dunkirk
and the Fall of France, Hitler had moved with apparent
infallibility. After Churchill, Hitler was "off" for good,
never regaining his sense of timing or his uncanny ability
to anticipate every opponent's slightest move. The shrewd
calculator of the 'thirties became the wild, uncontrolled
plunger of the 'forties. It is hard to realize today, thirty
years after the event, that without Churchill the United
States might well have resigned itself to Nazi domination
of Europe and of the still largely intact colonial empires
of Europe. Indeed even Russia might well not have resisted the Nazi invaders had not Churchill, a year earlier,
broken the Nazi spell. What Churchill gave was precisely
what Europe needed: moral authority, belief in values,
and faith in the rightness of rational action.

But this is hindsight. Churchill appears in *The End of
Economic Man* and is treated with great respect. Indeed,
reading now what I then wrote, I suspect that I secretly
hoped that Winston Churchill would indeed emerge into
leadership. I also never fell for the *ersatz* leaders such as
Marshal Pétain to whom a good many well-informed
contemporaries—a good many members of Roosevelt's
entourage in Washington, for instance—looked for deliv-
erance. Yet, in 1939, Churchill was a might-have-been: a

powerless old man rapidly approaching 70; a Cassandra who bored his listeners in spite (or perhaps because) of his impassioned rhetoric; a two-time loser who, however magnificent in opposition, had proven himself inadequate to the demands of office. I know that it is hard to believe today that even in 1940 Churchill was by no means the inevitable successor when the "Men of Munich" were swept out of office by the Fall of France and the retreat at Dunkirk. But we do know now that several other men were considered as prime ministers and that one or two of them actually had the "inside track" and almost got the appointment.

Churchill's emergence in 1940, more than a year after this book was first published, was the reassertion of the basic moral and political values for which *The End of Economic Man* had prayed and hoped. But all one could do in 1939 was pray and hope. The reality was the absence of leadership, the absence of affirmation, the absence of men of values and principle.

Hannah Arendt published in 1951 a book called *The Origins of Totalitarianism*. It is a distinguished work on the history of ideas, and a moving one. But it is remarkably apolitical, indeed antipolitical, dealing almost exclusively with the decay and disintegration of the metaphysical systems of German classical philosophy. Dr. Arendt identifies as one of the central weaknesses of the European, and especially the German intellectual, his disdain for the reality of society and government and his disinterest in power and the political process. But she

fully shares the tendency she herself deplores. Yet hers
is the only book, other than *The End of Economic Man*, to
concern itself at all with the question: "what caused totalitarianism and what made it prevail?"

Not that we lack books on the Europe of the 'twenties,
the 'thirties, or the 'forties. No other period in history has
called forth the flood of printed paper—memoirs and
biographies; detailed monographs on election campaigns
and on the myriad international conferences of the period; books on campaigns, commanders, theaters of war
and battles. There are more than one hundred books alone
on German-Russian relations in the two years between
the signing of the alliance between the two countries and
Hitler's invasion of Russia in June, 1941.

But there has not been one single attempt (except for
The End of Economic Man) to *explain* the rise of totalitarianism. There has been not one attempt to explain totalitarianism as a political and social phenomenon or to
analyze the dynamics of its rise to political and military
dominance. Yet surely, no other event of recent Western
history calls out more for analysis and explanation than
the sudden emergence of a political creed that denies
every single political value of the European tradition,
and of a political system that, for the first time, at least
in the West, totally denies the individual altogether.

What I have called here the "realities" of the 'thirties
—the assumption of a Europe-centered world; the perva-
siveness of a rotting Marxism; and the absence of leadership of even medium competency—may in large part

account for this signal silence. We have been, until now, far too close in time to these years to treat them as "history" and with detachment. After all, we, the generation over thirty today—and particularly those over fifty who are still occupying the command positions in politics, society, and economics—were actors or at least victims. All our lives have been molded by these years. Instead of asking, "what did really happen?" we still ask, "how could we have prevented it from happening?" We are still trying to undo the past rather than to explain it. Yet we are also so far removed in experience from these years that we cannot imagine their "realities." They do not make sense to us. They cannot fit in with the way we now see the world, with what we now take for granted, with what we now *know*.

These years are, therefore, to us like a nightmare the morning after. We still suffer from it, may indeed never be able to shake it off. But we no longer suffer with it. It has rather become incomprehensible to us how we could ever have succumbed. And this inhibits understanding, makes it even appear silly to try to gain understanding. For how can one explain or understand the totally meaningless?

Today, however, the generation for whom the interwar period, and especially the 'thirties, are still "contemporary," the generation that lives in the morning after the nightmare, is rapidly moving out. To anyone now thirty or under, this period is already impersonal, that is, "history." To them, therefore, the question how to *explain* the period is a meaningful, an accessible, perhaps even an important question. To them, the attempt made in *The End of Economic Man* might, therefore, make sense again.

Another reason why there has been no attempt to understand and explain the totalitarianism of the 'thirties, since *The End of Economic Man* first appeared, is probably that the attempt seemed unnecessary. We thought we were finished and done with this particular disease. This belief was not only common in the West and applied to Hitler and his Nazis. In Russia too most people are apparently convinced that "the Stalin years can never come back again." There are, God knows, enough dangers and horrors in the nineteen-sixties. But the totalitarianisms of a Hitler and of a Stalin, those, it seemed to us, were surely not among them. And what point is there in puzzling over something that will never come back?

But can we still be sure? Or are there not signs around us that totalitarianism may re-infest us, may indeed overwhelm us again? The problems of our times are very different from those of the 'twenties and 'thirties, and so are our realities. But some of our reactions to these problems are ominously reminiscent of the "despair of the masses" that plunged Europe into Hitler's totalitarianism and into World War II. In their behavior some groups—the racists, white and black, but also some of the student "activists" on the so-called Left—are frighteningly reminiscent of Hitler's stormtroopers—in their refusal to grant any rights, free speech for instance, to anyone else; in their use of character assassination; in their joy in destruction and vandalism. In their rhetoric these groups are odiously similar to Hitler's speeches and so is the dreary nihilism of their prophets of hatred from Mao to Marcuse. Their direct ancestors are the German "Youth Movement" of the years between 1910 and 1930—long hair, guitars, folk songs and all; and we might remember that the German Youth Movement started out as idealist "socialism" and ended up supplying Hitler with his most fanatical hard-core followers. But above all, these groups on the "Right" as well as on the "Left," like the totalitarians of a generation ago, believe that to say "no" is a positive policy; that to have compassion is to be weak; and that to manipulate idealism for the pursuit of power is to be "idealistic." They have not learned the one great lesson of our recent past: hatred is no answer to despair.

The End of Economic Man does not attempt to analyze the problems of today. The problems with which it deals are clearly yesterday, clearly history, clearly thirty years ago. But it does show that evasion of these problems through flight into righteous nihilism leads to the paranoia of tyranny.

The totalitarian response, this book shows, does not solve anything. On the contrary, the problems are only made much worse, and the world made more nightmarish. To be sure, this world of ours—like probably all societies before—is insane. But paranoia is not the cure for an insane world. On the contrary, what is needed to make life bearable in an insane environment is sanity. Matu-

rity, to use a much abused word, does not consist of trying
to make the universe rational. That attempt, the attempt
of the nineteenth century, will probably always end in
frustration. Maturity does, however, not consist either of
trying to outdo the irrationality of the universe. It requires
that we make our own behavior rational—and this alone
gives us the chance at a decent, a meaningful, an achiev-
ing life and a decent society.

In *The End of Economic Man* I did not attempt to defend the society of the 'twenties or to explain away its
problems, its ills, its evils. But I did try to show the consequences of a total repudiation of the "establishment"
(a term we did not know thirty years ago, of course), the
consequences of believing that "no" by itself is an adequate answer, or indeed an answer at all. Understanding
of the dynamics of the totalitarianism of yesterday may
help us better to understand today and to prevent a recur-
rence of yesterday. It may, I hope above all, help young
people today to turn their idealism, their genuine distress
over the horrors of this world, and their desire for a better
and braver tomorrow into constructive action *for*, rather
than into totalitarian nihilism as their predecessors did
thirty years ago. For at the end of this road there could
only be another Hitler and another "ultimate solution"
with its gas chambers and extermination camps.

Though published thirty years ago, *The End of Economic Man* is still being widely read and quoted. But I
believe that the time has come to re-issue this book and
to make it available to a wider reading public, especially,

of course, to the young people most of whom were not even born when it first came out. My own work has led me into many other fields: the study of the new organizations of our pluralist society—government agency, business corporation, trade union, hospital, and so on—their structure and management; the anticipation and analysis of trends in knowledge, learning, and perception; and the opportunities, needs and careers of the educated young people in our "educated society." Yet *The End of Economic Man* may, of all my books, be the one most particularly relevant to young people today. It should not only help them understand what we, their parents, should have understood to avert the great catastrophe of our lives. It may help today's generation avert another such catastrophe in their own lives.

PETER F. DRUCKER

Montclair, New Jersey
New Year's Day, 1969

FOREWORD

THIS IS A political book. As such it does not lay claim to the detached aloofness of the scholar nor to the studied impartiality of the news reporter. It has a political purpose to serve: to strengthen the will to maintain freedom against the threat of its abandonment in favor of totalitarianism. And it is based upon the preconceived conviction that there can be no compromise between the basic principles of the European tradition and those of the totalitarian revolution.

Just because I am aware that fascism and Nazism threaten the basic principles of Europe, I have found myself unable to accept the usual explanations and interpretations of the totalitarian revolution. They appear to me to content themselves with surface phenomena. Only too often they refuse to admit unassailable evidence and cling instead to wishful thinking in a way pathetically reminiscent of the self-deception in which all *ancien régime*'s have indulged in order to conceal that they had actually died. And this self-deception of the advocates of the old order has always helped the new revolutionary forces more than their own victories.

It has therefore seemed imperative to me to find an explanation and interpretation of totalitarianism which is valid and adequate. Since there are neither "accidents" nor "miracles" in political and social life, and since political and social effects always have adequate causes, a revolution that threatens the basis of society can only be explained by fundamental changes within the basis of social organization itself. It must be owing to a revolution of man's concept of his own nature, of the nature of his society, and of his own function and place in this society.

In this book I have made an attempt to explain and interpret fascism and Nazism as fundamental revolutions. This analysis confines itself intentionally to the social and economic sphere, though I do not believe in the materialist interpretation of history. I believe that the material, far from being the foundation of human society, is but one pole of human existence. It is of no greater, though of no less, importance than the other pole, the spiritual—corresponding to man's dual nature as belonging at the same time to the animal kingdom and to the kingdom of heaven. Accordingly human developments and changes show as much in man's spiritual activity and in the arts as in society and business; to analyze a revolution would seem to call for an analysis of the whole. But, in the first place, such an attempt is bound to come to grief and to end in a Spenglerian nightmare which, though it may not have overlooked the least little detail of human activity—cooking or sex rites, military tactics or cartography—has yet lost track of man himself in the process. In the second place, the last centuries have been characterized by their efforts to make the spiritual serve the material sphere. It would clearly be the most roundabout and wasteful way to try, for instance, to analyze the religious Reformation of the sixteenth century as originating in the social and economic sphere since the preceding centuries from the thirteenth onward had been characterized by the attempted subordination of the material to the spiritual sphere. But it would be equally wasteful to start an analysis of the present revolution from the spiritual sphere. Nevertheless, it should not be forgotten that my analysis of the changes in the social sphere gives only one-half of the picture.

My attempts to formulate this analysis go back to the halcyon days of pre-Hitler Europe when Italian fascism seemed to be just a negligible annoyance in a democratic world which was fast approaching perfection. But even then our peace of mind seemed unreal, and some catastrophe imminent. This analysis had, accordingly, been completed in substance when Nazism came to power in Germany. It has stood the test of the years since, in so far as it has enabled me to forecast the actual trend of events with some degree of exactitude. Since I can claim, therefore, that it has proved itself to be more than a mere hypothesis, I feel justified in publishing it.

Doing so, however, I feel compelled to add one warning which seems so important to me that I repeat it in the book itself. Though this analysis has been written in New York, and though it is intended primarily for American readers, its conclusions are not to be applied indiscriminately—if at all—to the United States. Whatever the underlying forces are which will determine the developments in the United States, they are different from those in Europe. The tendency to apply European patterns to American developments to which only too many of my American friends are prone, seems to me to be detrimental to the understanding of Europe as well as to that of the United States. It would, indeed, run counter to all my intentions if my arguments and conclusions were to be used—or abused—for similar purposes.

Finally, I should like to express my gratitude to my wife, who has aided and assisted me throughout my work with advice, criticism, and suggestions. I should never have been able to complete it but for her help and co-operation. I should also like to record my indebtedness to Mr. Richard J. Walsh, who has revised the entire manuscript, and whose suggestions and recommendations have proved invaluable; and to Mr. Harold Manheim, who has given lavishly of his time and advice in connection with the final editing.

PETER F. DRUCKER

Bronxville, New York
January, 1939

THE END OF ECONOMIC MAN

CHAPTER ONE

THE ANTI-FASCIST ILLUSION

WITHIN a few short years fascist totalitarianism has assumed the proportions of a major world revolution. It has become the only effective political force in Europe, and has reduced democracy to impotent defense internally and externally. Fascist ideology and phraseology are accepted as a cloak by divergent and incongruous movements all over the world. The new nationalism in the Near East, the old feudalism of the Far East, traditional *coup d'état's* and "racial awakenings" in Latin America, religious revolts in the Asiatic or African colonial empires call themselves "totalitarian" in the same way in which such movements would have sailed thirty years ago under the democratic, and ten years ago under the communist, flag. And communism—the world revolution of yesterday—has not only been forced to admit that it has become purely defensive, but also that it has lost its fight. Whatever mental reservations the communist leaders might have made regarding the distant future, their drive for a united front with the bourgeoisie and with capitalist democracy against fas-

3

cism amounts to complete abdication as a revolutionary
force, and to virtual renunciation of the promise to be
harbingers of the future social order. The impotence of
the "popular front" in France, and the complete collapse
of the united front idea altogether over the Czechoslovak
crisis, meant the end of communism as an effective resistance to fascism.

The rapid ascendancy of totalitarianism is all the
more spectacular in view of the general hostility which
it meets abroad. Everywhere there is nothing but horror
of its brutality, fear of its aggressiveness, revulsion from
its slogans and its gospel of hate. Unlike any earlier
revolution, not even the minority in the countries of the
old order accepts the tenets, the spirit, and the achievements of totalitarianism. And yet, fascism has been gaining ground steadily until it has become master of Europe.

Why has the solid opposition of the democracies been
unable to check this greatest danger to all they believe
in? It cannot have been cowardice. The heroism of the
thousands who have laid down their lives in Spain for
the sake of fighting fascism, of the Austrian workers
who sacrificed themselves, or of the unsung, anonymous
underground workers in Italy and Germany, is beyond
doubt. If courage could have stopped totalitarianism it
would have been stopped.

The reason why all resistance to the fascist menace
has proved unavailing is that we do not know what we

fight. We know the symptoms of fascism, but we do not know its causes and its meaning. And the very people who have made resistance to fascism the main article of their creed by calling themselves anti-Fascists insist upon fighting a phantom of their own invention. This ignorance is the main cause, both of the complacent hope of one section of public opinion in the democratic countries that the "radicalism" of fascism is but a passing phase and of the anti-fascist illusion that fascism "cannot last," which together have been responsible for the ineffectiveness of democratic resistance. The analysis of the causes of fascism would therefore appear to be our most important task.

The attempt to understand rationally the phenomenon of fascism is not, as is frequently asserted by people whose emotion gets the better of their judgment, a defense of and apology for fascism, but on the contrary the only basis from which a successful fight against its world-wide spread can be waged.

As a revolution which threatens every concept on which European civilization has been based, fascism has its roots in European developments. To what extent the same forces which produced fascism in Europe are effective and active in the United States as well, I am not qualified to determine. But I firmly believe that this country is so dissimilar and contains such strong independent forces of its own as to make invalid any direct application of my conclusions to American conditions. I hope that this analysis of the causes and of the meaning of fascism will serve a real purpose in this country; but not that of inducing my American readers to apply European clichés to their own country.

Apart from the assertion that the majority of the people in the fascist countries are secretly hostile to the regime and are only held down by terror, which is such a flagrant perversion of all evidence as to require no specific refutation, three explanations of the nature of fascism are generally offered: (1) fascism is a malicious outbreak of primitive barbarity and brutality; or (2) it is a temporarily successful attempt of the capitalists to delay or to prevent the final, inevitable victory of socialism; or (3) it is the result of the impact of unscrupulous and technically perfect propaganda upon the gullible masses and their basest instincts.

Every one of these assertions is meaningless as an explanation of the nature and the causes of totalitarianism. It is certainly true that fascism excels in sanguinary brutality and wanton cruelty, and that it tramples on life and liberty of the individual. In the eyes of the writer, who believes in an absolute good and evil, this alone would be sufficient reason to condemn fascism in its entirety. But it does not explain anything. Brutality and cruelty are in themselves only symptoms that fascism is a revolution which, like all revolutions, shakes men out of their customary routine tracks and releases their hidden ferocious instincts. Brutality, cruelty, and bloodshed are characteristics of every revolution, regardless of its causes, nature, and direction. The forces of destruction are as evil as they are blind.

As for the explanation that fascism is a last desperate attempt of capitalism to delay the socialist revolution, it simply is not true. It is not true that "big business" promoted fascism. On the contrary, both in Italy and in Germany the proportion of fascist sympathizers and backers was smallest in the industrial and banking classes. It is equally untrue that "big business" profits from fascism; of all the classes it probably suffers most from totalitarian economics and *Wehrwirtschaft*. And finally, it is just ridiculous to maintain that the capitalist class—or, for that matter, anybody else—had reason to fear a victory of the working classes in pre-fascist Italy and Germany. The whole thesis is nothing but a feeble attempt to reconcile Marxist theory with the facts by falsifying history; it is a lame apology but not a serious explanation.

The most dangerous and at the same time most stupid explanation of fascism is the propaganda theory. In the first place, I have never been able to find anyone who could reconcile it with the fact that right up to the fascist victory—and in Italy beyond it—literally all means of propaganda were in the hands of uncompromising

enemies of fascism. There was not one widely-read newspaper but poured ridicule on Hitler and Mussolini while
the Nazi and the fascist press were unread and on the
verge of bankruptcy. The radio in Germany, owned by
the government, issued one anti-Nazi broadside after the
other. More powerful than both, the established churches
used all the enormous direct influence of the pulpit and
of the confessional to fight fascism and Nazism.

But this is a minor matter compared to the short-
sightedness which can deceive itself into using as an
argument *against* fascism that the masses have been
doped by propaganda. For this would be an argument
only in support of fascism; and Hitler has indeed used
it as such in his *Mein Kampf*. In fighting against fascism
we profess to fight for democracy and freedom, for individual liberty and for the inalienable rights and dignity of man. If we ourselves admit that the masses can
be lured by propaganda to give up these rights, there
can be no justification at all for our creed and we had
better become fascists ourselves. This would at least be
more sincere and less harmful than the pretentiousness
of the fake aristocratism which, while bemoaning the decline of freedom and liberty, fears the "revolt of the
masses."

But to deny liberty and self-determination to the
masses in order to shield them from propaganda is no
alternative to fascism; nor would absence of propaganda

have prevented its spread. Learned scholars in learned books on mass psychology have come to the conclusion that it is owing only to the chance absence of the right type of demagogic mass-leader that we do not go on all fours or are not all nudists, since the masses "provably" fall easy prey to any superior salesman, whatever his goods. Yet it is as true today as it ever was that propaganda only converts those who already believe, and only appeals to people if it answers an existing need or allays an existing fear. The success of a certain type of propaganda and its reasons are valuable symptoms. But propaganda is not a cause, nor is counterpropaganda a cure.

That the anti-fascist movements content themselves with these attempts at explanation—partly untrue, partly meaningless, always superficial—is not just an accident. It is the logical result of their fundamental self-deception and delusion. They refuse to see and to realize that the "total state" of fascism is not a political alignment *within* the existing political and social setup, but that it is a revolution which, like all revolutions, works from *without*. To the anti-fascist the world is still unchanged in its essentials and fascism must fit in somehow. Actually, fascism has already changed or destroyed those essentials of yesterday, as is shown by the fact that every nation would have to go totalitarian in the event of war. For, as long as war remains a means of politics, any radical change in the social organization of warfare such as has been wrought by "total war" with its new weapons and its new concept of belligerents, indicates a profound revolutionary change in the social and political order.

The illusion that a revolution is not a revolution, but one of the old forces in a new disguise, has always been entertained by the *ancien régime*. That only a small minority supports the new movement and that, moreover, its victories are entirely due to rabble-rousing and to the stirring-up of the basest instincts, was held as stubbornly by the Popes in the sixteenth century as by the Cavaliers in the seventeenth and by the French aristocracy in the eighteenth. This illusion has always been the main reason why the forces of the old order were defeated. A revolution can only be overcome if it is recognized as such and if its true causes are diagnosed correctly. And the true cause, the only possible cause, of a revolution is a fundamental and radical change in the order of values, especially in that most important sphere, man's conception of his own nature and of his place in the universe and in society.

If we want to understand what distinguishes fascism from the revolutions of the past, we have to start with the symptoms which are new and particular to it. Therefore we can disregard its terror, its ruthless persecution of dissenters and minorities, and its cruelty and brutality as typical of revolutions in general. The same holds true of the outward form of military dictatorship and even of the fact that the dictator came from below and did not belong to the "polite society" of the old order. Finally, contrary to general opinion, the combination of "formal legality" and open illegality of the revolutionary movement has been common in some degree to all European revolutions ever since centralized government replaced feudal decentralization long before Cromwell.

The novel and therefore dfferentiating symptoms are threefold:

(1) Fascist totalitarianism has no positive ideology, but confines itself to refuting, fighting, and denying all traditional ideas and ideologies.

(2) Fascism not only refutes all old ideas but denies, for the first time in European history, the foundation on which all former political and social systems had been built: the justification of the social and political system and of the authority constituted under it as the only means to further the true well-being of the individual subjected to it.

(3) The masses joined fascism not because they believe in its promises, which take the place of a positive creed, but *because they do not believe in them.*

We have the testimony of Mussolini himself, who repeatedly boasted that fascism, when it came to power, had no positive policy, no program, and no system. Only afterwards were the historians and philosophers commissioned to fashion an ideology. Hitler is less frank and probably also less clearheaded; but the positive creed of Nazism: the worship of the old Germanic gods, the Nordic perfect man, the corporate state composed of self-governing, autonomous "estates," and the heroic family, has remained in the books. The masses are not interested in these concepts and ideas; not even the best-organized mass meeting shows any enthusiasm for them. And it was certainly not these mystical new articles of faith which brought frenzied mass support to Hitler.

Mussolini—and Hitler, imitating him—have tried to make an asset out of the lack of a positive creed and a system out of having none. That, and nothing else, is the meaning of Mussolini's "men make history"! Insofar as this was meant to read, "Mussolini makes history," the slogan is neither particularly original nor in any way important. But Mussolini meant much more: he wanted to claim that the deed is before the thought, and that revolution logically precedes the development of a new creed or of a new economic order. Historically, this is nonsense. All revolutions of the past have been caused by protracted and profound developments either in the intellectual sphere or in the social, or in both. The "great historical figure" at best provided the ignition and was often only a tool. Mussolini's contention is, however, correct—or partly correct—insofar as it applies to the fascist and Nazi revolutions. There the "deed"—i.e., the revolution—took place without the previous development of a positive creed or of a new socio-economic order.

But if there is no positive creed in totalitarianism, there is as compensation an abundance of negatives. Of course, every revolution repudiates what went on before and considers itself a conscious break with the past; it is only posterity that sees, or imagines it sees, the historical continuity. Fascism, however, goes much further in its negation of the past than any earlier political movement, because it makes this negation its main platform. What is even more important, it denies simultaneously ideas and tendencies which are in themselves antithetic. It is antiliberal, but also anticonservative; antireligious and antiatheist; anticapitalist and antisocialist; antiwar and antipacifist; against big business, but also against the small artisans and shopkeepers who are regarded as superfluous—the list could be continued indefinitely. It is typical that the leitmotiv of all Nazi propaganda is not the "Nordic man," not the promises, conquests, and achievements of Nazism, but *anti-Semitism,* the attack against the "fourteen years" before Hitler and against foreign conspiracy. The Nazi agitator whom, many years ago, I heard proclaim to a wildly cheering peasants' meeting: *"We don't want lower bread prices, we don't want higher bread prices, we don't want unchanged bread* prices—*we want National-Socialist bread prices,*" came nearer explaining fascism than anybody I have heard since. But for the sentimental invocation of the glory of the Rome of the Caesars, which is anyhow too far away to be a living tradition, Italian fascism works in the same way.

Of these denials of European tradition one is especially important: that is the refutation of the demand that the political and social order and the authority set up under it have to justify themselves as benefiting their subjects. Hardly any other concept or idea of our past is held up to so much ridicule by fascism as that of the justification of power. "Power is its own justification" is regarded as self-evident. Nothing shows better how far the totalitarian revolution has already gone than the general acceptance of this new maxim throughout Europe as a matter of course. Actually it is the most startling innovation. For the last two thousand years, ever since Aristotle, the justification of power and authority has been the central problem of European political thought and of European political history. And since Europe became Christian there has never been any other approach to this problem than that of seeking justification in the benefit which the exercise of power confers upon its subjects—be it the salvation of their souls, the "good life," or the highest standard of living for the greatest number. Not even the most fanatical advocate of absolute monarchy would have dared to justify the sovereign otherwise. The German Protestant clerics of the sixteenth century who developed the idea of the divine right of autocracy, as well as Hobbes and Bossuet, took the greatest pains to prove the benefits for the subjects. The infinite contempt in which Machiavelli has been held by contemporaries and posterity is entirely due to his indifference to the moral justification of authority, which made this conscientious and honest man appear a moral leper even in the corrupt and power-obsessed world of the Italian Renaissance. In every social system that bases itself on the European tradition, the justification of power must be the central problem. For it is through this concept alone that freedom and equality—or, as was formerly said, justice—can be projected into the social and political reality; and freedom and equality have been Europe's basic spiritual ideas ever since the introduction of Christianity. But to fascism the problem does not even exist except as a ridiculous relic of "Jewish liberalism."

Even more important as a symptom of the true nature of fascism is the psychology of its appeal to the masses. The emphasis laid upon the "propaganda" explanation by practically all students of the problem—fascist and others—implicitly recognizes its importance. The maxim that "a lie becomes accepted as the truth if it is only repeated often enough" would seem to be an obvious and easily understandable explanation; but it happens to be the wrong one. Nothing impressed me more in Germany in the years before Hitler than the almost universal disbelief in the Nazi promises and the indifference toward the Nazi creed among the most fanatical Nazis. Outside the party ranks this disbelief turned into open ridicule. And yet the masses flocked to the Nazi fold.

One example—the case of the Boxheim Documents—shows to the full the inner contradiction of the belief in Nazi propaganda. Some time before Hitler came to power a memorandum in which a group of young Nazis had tried to formulate their picture of the coming Nazi state became public through an indiscretion. They had followed closely the official party program, Hitler's speeches, and his book. The result was a forecast that has proved astonishingly correct. Yet, although no other conclusion could have been reached on the basis of the Nazi tenets, the publication of the document provoked boundless laughter—in the Nazi ranks. I talked at the time with a great number of convinced Nazis—students, small shopkeepers, white-collar workers, and unemployed—and there was not one but was sincerely convinced that the thing was an absurdity and that only the most stupid and most ignorant person could really believe that the Nazi creed and the Nazi tenets could or would be realized. "Life under such conditions would be impossible and unbearable" was the unanimous and sin-

cere conclusion of all these devoted Nazis, every one of
whom was ready to die for the party.

Equally striking is the fact that racial anti-Semitism
was not taken seriously even by the great majority of
Nazis. "It is just a catchword to attract voters" was a
standing phrase which everybody repeated and believed,
and that I took it seriously was more than once regarded
as definite proof of my stupidity and gullibility.

The same contradiction appeared in the vital issue of
war or peace. That the German people feared war as
much as any other nation in Europe was undoubtedly
true before 1933, and it is hardly less true today. It was
obvious to everyone that Hitler's foreign policy must
mean war in the long run. Yet every Nazi believed and
still believes Hitler's protestations of his peaceful intentions.

The masses must have known that Hitler's promises
were incompatible each with the other. They may have
been taken in in spiritual matters such as the simultaneity
of rabid anti-Christian propaganda with equally fervent
assertions that Nazism is the savior of the churches. But
German farmers trained by a hundred years of co-opera-
tive organization, and German workers after sixty years
of trade-unionism and collective bargaining, could not
have failed to notice the glaring conflict between simultaneous promises—such as, for instance, those made by
Dr. Goebbels in one and the same speech in 1932—that

the farmer would receive more for his grain, the worker pay less for his bread, and the baker and grocer have a higher wholesale and retail margin. And what about the Berlin metal-workers' strike in 1932—one of the most embittered labor conflicts in German history—when the Nazis together with the Communists supported the strike against the official trade unions who had called it off, while Hitler at the very same moment promised the extremely class-conscious metal manufacturers in a public speech that under Nazism they would again be master in their own house? Result: half the workers and almost all the industrialists turned Nazi. Yet no propaganda could have made employers in the Berlin metal industry or German workers overlook or forget such a contradiction. Or what about Hitler's oath in court that his movement relied entirely on "legal means," while at the same time he made some Nazis "honorary members of the Party" in an enthusiastic telegram reprinted everywhere, as a reward for having murdered an unarmed and defenseless opponent?

Nor should it be forgotten that these astonishing feats were witnessed by a hostile press, a hostile radio, a hostile cinema, a hostile church, and a hostile government which untiringly pointed out the Nazi lies, the Nazi inconsistency, the unattainability of their promises, and the dangers and folly of their course. Clearly, nobody would have been a Nazi if rational belief in the Nazi promises had been a prerequisite.

In addition, the Nazi leaders themselves never pretended to speak the truth. Beginning with Hitler's frank admission in his book that lying is necessary, Nazi leaders have prided themselves publicly on their disregard for truth and on the impossibility of their promises —foremost among them Dr. Goebbels. Not once but several times have I heard him say in mass meetings when the people cheered a particularly choice lie: "Of course, you understand all this is just propaganda"; and the masses only cheered louder.

The same thing happened in Austria; the same thing in Czechoslovakia; the same thing, I understand, with slight modifications, in pre-fascist Italy. Is there any other explanation than that the masses believed in fascism although—or perhaps even because—they did not believe its promises?

These three main characteristics peculiar to fascism: the absence of a positive creed and the overemphasis on the refutation of the whole past, the denial of the demand for the justification of power, and the trust of the masses in fascism in spite of their lack of belief in its statements and promises, are the symptoms on which any serious diagnosis has to be based. They are in themselves symptoms only, though important ones, and they do not explain fascism. But they show where the disease is located, and they indicate the order and species to which it belongs.

Of the three, the first is easiest to understand and to place. The overemphasis on the negative is clearly meant to offset the absence of a positive creed. It shows that, in spite of Mussolini and Hitler, deeds do not come before thought, but that a revolution has to have a creed; if a genuinely positive new creed is unavailable, the negative must be substituted. This means that the fascist revolution, like all European revolutions, has its roots in developments in the spiritual, intellectual, and social field and not, as the Fascists themselves pretend, in that of action. There is only one fundamental difference to the usual—but not, as will be shown later, the invariable —pattern. In the typical revolution the old orders, systems, and creeds break down simultaneously with the emergence of a new order. The fascist revolution, like all its predecessors, has been caused by the breakdown of the old order from within. But in marked contrast to historical precedent no new positive creed appeared as soon as the old one collapsed.

This supplies also the explanation for the fascist attitude toward the justification of power which has been the mainstay of all orders and creeds of the European past. There can be no doubt that fascism, which suffers so acutely from the lack of a positive creed, would have availed itself of a solution continuing the European tradition, had one existed. The break with freedom and equality and with the justification of power implies, therefore, that there is, at least at present, no way to continue the European tradition and to derive a new solution from it. Inability to develop the European basic concepts any further in the direction in which they had been moving the last few hundred years must obviously be the fundamental cause of fascism.

This assumption is supported by our third symptom: the psychology of the attraction of fascism, which also elucidates the nature of its new solution. At first sight this psychology might appear as something most extraordinary and complicated. But in ordinary life we meet it all the time, and we know without difficulty what it means if somebody believes against belief. The small boy who has smashed the jar while stealing the jam knows that he will be discovered and punished; but he prays, hopes, and believes against belief that he will escape. During the last few years the British Government has been doing the same thing. It knows that there is no lasting peace with the dictators; but it believes against belief, hopes against hope, that it can be found. Both the boy and the British Government hope for a miracle. The boy hopes for the intervention of his guardian angel or for a nice fire that would cover up his tracks by burning the house. The British Government, since it is composed of mature men, asks fate for much more unlikely miracles: it hopes for a revolution in Germany, an economic smash-up, or a Russo-German war. Both make themselves believe in a miracle against all reason and knowledge because the alternative is too terrible to face. Both turn to the miracle because they are in despair. And so are the masses when they turn to fascism.

The old orders have broken down, and no new order can be contrived from the old foundations. The alternative is chaos; and in despair the masses turn to the magician who promises to make the impossible possible: to make the workers free and simultaneously to make the industrialist "master in his own house"; to increase the price of wheat and at the same time to lower the price of bread; to bring peace, yet to bring victory in war; to be everything to everybody and all things to all men. So it is not in spite of but because of its contradictions and its impossibility that the masses turn to fascism. For if you are caught between the flood of a past, through which you cannot retrace your steps, and an apparently unscalable blank wall in front of you, it is only by magic and miracles that you can hope to escape. *Credo quia absurdum,* that cry of a master who had known all the bitterness of deepest and blackest despair, is heard again for the first time in many a century.

The despair of the masses is the key to the understanding of fascism. No "revolt of the mob," no "triumphs of unscrupulous propaganda," but stark despair caused by the breakdown of the old order and the absence of a new one.

What broke down? Why and how? What miracle has fascism to fulfill? How does it try and can it do it? Will there be a new order? When and on what basis? These questions I have to answer in the following analysis. I will anticipate only one point: the abracadabra of fascism is the substitution of *organization* for creed and order; though it cannot succeed and cannot last, the formal democracy of capitalism and of socialism cannot prevent its spread. But the glorification of organization as an end in itself shows that eventually there will be a new order based upon a reformulation of the old fundamental values of European tradition: freedom and equality.

CHAPTER TWO

THE DESPAIR OF THE MASSES

FASCISM is the result of the collapse of Europe's spiritual and social order. The last, decisive step leading to this collapse was the disintegration of the belief in Marxist socialism, which has been proved unable to overcome capitalism and to establish a new order.

The failure of Marxism does not lie in the economic sphere. The argument that it has never been tried anywhere under the "right economic conditions" simply has nothing to do with the real issue. Nor are the squabbles and discussions between Marxist and non-Marxist economists important or relevant in any respect. Marxist economics might result in an increase in production, wealth, and consumption which would give to every proletarian goods and luxuries such as no millionaire can afford today; and yet Marxism would have been effectively and completely disproved, and the belief in it would have disintegrated. On the other hand, even complete economic failure resulting in rapid impoverishment and stark misery would not have been able to shake the belief in the Marxist creed if only the social promise of Marxism appeared to be capable of realization.

Marxism stands and falls by the promise to overcome the unequal and unfree society of capitalism and to realize freedom and equality in the classless society. And it is because it has been proved that it cannot attain the classless society but must necessarily lead to an even more rigid and unfree pattern of classes that Marxist socialism has ceased to be a creed. From being the gospel of the future order which promises to overcome the inequities of capitalism by revolution, it has degenerated into a mere opposition within capitalism. As such it is highly effective. But a movement which exhausts itself in opposition derives its appeal and validity from the system which it opposes. Since criticism is its only function, socialism as a social force is necessarily dependent upon the existence and validity of capitalism. Socialism can weaken the belief in capitalism; it cannot replace it. When capitalism disintegrates, socialism ceases to have any validity or justification.

The one fundamental socialist dogma without which belief in the order of Marxism is impossible, is that capitalism in its trend toward larger and larger producing units must by necessity develop a social structure in which all are equal as proletarians except a few expropriators. The expropriation of those few would then usher in the classless society. In other words, while the producing unit will become necessarily larger, the number of privileged unequals will become necessarily smaller, and finally the conversion of the whole productive machinery into one unit, owned and operated by and for the community of workers, will be inevitable and will eliminate inequality and privilege altogether. Actually, however, the number of privileged unequals increases in almost geometrical proportion to the size of the producing unit. The number of independent "bosses" decreases, of course, especially if the individual small stockholder in a large company is not regarded as independent, since he has no control. But the larger the unit becomes, the larger is the number of intermediate privileged positions, the holders of which are not independent entrepreneurs but even less unequal members of the proletariat. Between the overpaid president of a large company and the worst-paid ledger clerk, from the chief designer to the semiskilled foreman on an assembly line, there has come into existence a veritable army of dependent bourgeois classes. None of them has that interest in the "expropriated profit" which characterizes the "bourgeois" in Marxism. But all have a vested interest in the maintenance of unequal society. With the complete socialization of productive capacity, the number, size, and rigidity of these privileged though employed intermediate layers and classes would increase so tremendously as to crowd out the unskilled laborer at the bottom, in whose name and for whose nominal benefit the rapidly multiplying bureaucracy would be planning, designing, directing, and administrating the social and economic fabric. Economically the system might perform miracles of efficiency and productivity. But, far from being classless, it would be a society with the most rigid and most complicated pattern of naturally antagonistic classes which the world has ever seen. Instead of establishing the true freedom, the socialist state would produce a genuinely feudal society, though the serf would be proclaimed the beneficiary. In the heyday of feudalism in the twelfth and early thirteenth centuries the social pyramid was rationalized by the creed on which society was based. But social stratification in the socialist state cannot be justified. It cannot even be explained. It is as senseless as a hierarchy without God. That such a society is the inevitable consequence of the realization of socialism invalidated, therefore, all basis of belief in the Marxist creed as the harbinger of the future order.

Ever since Marx, the Marxists have been struggling with the problem of the middle class. But if they want to remain socialists they must shut their eyes to all implications except those of practical politics. The most recent attempt in this direction is the justification and explanation of the communist "united front" policy by Sidney Hook in the United States and by John Strachey in England. But to solve the problem merely as one of temporary political expediency is not to solve it at all. A problem does not become less important and less fundamental if you just deny its existence. Yet any approach that admits its fundamental importance destroys the belief in the socialist creed. The three most promising political philosophers of prewar Europe—the Frenchman Georges Sorel, the Italian Pareto, the German Robert Michels— all started as good Marxists to find a truly socialist fundamental solution of the problem, and came out as violent foes of Marxism and as intellectual and spiritual fathers of fascism.

In due deference to the genius of Marx, it must be said that he alone of all Marxists saw the problem as a fundamental one and yet remained a "Marxist." But he could remain consistent only because he formulated the problem as one of economic theory solely, and disregarded entirely its far more important social aspect. Even then he did not find an answer, but had to give up. The famous irreconcilable conflict between the two theories of value in the Marxist economic system had its cause in this very dilemma. It is none other than an economic formulation of the problem of the middle classes. The Marxist theory of value, which is the cornerstone of his economic system, declares that work alone produces value and that the ultimate value of a product is equal to the total quantity of work expended upon it. It follows that only work is productive, and that profit, constituting "workless income," is a spoliation of the worker. It also follows that all work is equally valuable and that all workers should be paid equally according to the physical effort expended. But Marx was also keenly aware that different skills make qualitatively different contributions toward the final value of the product. He realized that this leads to the justification of a privileged unequal class of petty bourgeois. Ultimately it even implies an economic justification of private profit on capital in industrial production.

Marx himself, as already said, gave up. His inability to solve the problem to his own satisfaction is generally held to be the reason why he did not write the concluding volume of *Das Kapital*. And yet he had not even touched upon the most important aspect: that the middle class becomes necessarily larger and more unequally privileged the further capitalism proceeds toward the "one-monopoly" stage. Modern mass production proved the industrial bureaucracy of bookkeepers, engineers, draftsmen, and buyers to be the most vital, most indispensable part of industrial production. Therewith the Marxist dream that a transfer in ownership abolishing the private entrepreneur would establish the classless society necessarily evaporated. With it perished the belief that the trend of all industry toward huge monopolies would "automatically" lead to the revolutionary change in ownership.

If socialism cannot establish the classless society its aims must of necessity become limited to improving the social and economic lot of the workers. It becomes trade-unionism. The change is not just one of technique and methods; it is a change of character and of fundamentals. Socialism that promises the inevitable classless society aims at a new order superseding capitalism after its "inevitable" and desirable fall. Consequently, it aims at the collapse of capitalism and welcomes any development leading to it. It is opposition to capitalism from without. Socialism that has become trade-unionism aims at the betterment of one class within capitalism. It fights to give this class the largest possible share, i.e., the largest share possible under capitalist methods of production. Anything that benefits the capitalist system as a whole benefits by necessity this trade-unionist socialist movement as it increases the total national income available for distribution among the classes. Socialism as an opposition from within is salutary and inevitable, but accepts necessarily the fundamentals of the capitalist social system.

The nearer capitalist economy approaches the stage at which, according to the socialist creed, it should become "ripe" for socialism, the more pronounced becomes this new character of the labor movement as a movement within capitalism. The most striking proof is the development in the United States where, in spite of many efforts,

the labor movements never turned socialist but consciously accepted the capitalist order. This is owing neither
to the youth of the country, nor to the wealth of opportunities to become independent, nor to the lack of class-
consciousness, but to the fact that the major industries in
the United States started as big business. In Europe the
labor movement began when industry was mostly in the
form of small shops in which the owner alone was privileged and unequal; consequently, the labor movement
started as a revolutionary socialist movement believing
in the attainability of a classless society through the
growth of industrialization. But as producing units grew
it shifted toward trade-unionism. Since railroading was
the first big business, the railroad workers were the first
to shift; they became everywhere the most conservative,
most procapitalist wing of the labor movement. The
workers in all the other industries followed. Then came
the shift from "revolution" to "evolution," to "reform"
and to protective social legislation, to participation in the
government of capitalist society and toward "industrial
democracy" as aims of socialism. Finally evolved the
"united front" with the bourgeoisie.

But the appeal of socialism had not been based originally upon its promise to bring better bargaining conditions for unskilled workers. It owed its strength and its
very existence as a creed to the promise to bring a new
social order and to establish equality. Without this ap-

peal the belief in socialism has no basis and disintegrates. Its continued existence becomes dependent upon the belief in the capitalist creed and the capitalist order of which it has become a part—though as integral opposition.

Marxist socialism can still be a creed in precapitalist and pre-industrial colonial or feudal countries such as pre-Bolshevik Russia, Spain, colonial Asia, and Latin America, where social conditions make the classless society appear feasible; a handful of landowners and entrepreneurs on the one side, the amorphous, equal, proletarian mass of the people on the other—and nothing in between. The masses might therefore still believe that they can establish the classless society of equals by the elimination of the few people who own anything at all. But the intermediary middle class is absent, not because society has completed the full cycle of capitalist development, but precisely because capitalism has not even started. This explains why, contrary to all Marxist creed, the socialist revolution did not start in the most highly developed industrial country in Europe but in the most backward one—in Russia, where there was really no economic and social substance on which to pin the Marxist pattern. It also explains why, contrary to all hopes of the communist leaders, the Russian revolution did not release at once the revolution in the West and in central Europe that was considered to be "due." Even the ablest

Marxist leaders failed to understand their own position. Lenin and Trotsky were absolutely convinced for almost six months in 1917 and early 1918 that the German and Austrian masses would rise in socialist revolution, once Russia had given the signal. They were so sure that they not only delayed the peace negotiations with Germany at the risk of an armed rising behind their backs, but insisted—Trotsky till now—that their revolution was "Russian" only by accident—almost, so to speak, by mistake—and that it was an Austrian or German revolution by design, necessity, and meaning.

This also explains why no adherent of socialism can interpret to his or anybody else's satisfaction the developments following the revolutions in Russia, Spain, Mexico, or in any other precapitalist country that should adopt socialism. Immediately the very phenomenon appears which makes impossible the realization of the classless society of socialism: the unequal privileged middle classes. The process of industrialization and socialization which logically and inevitably follows the successful revolution, leads as logically and inevitably to the emergence of the same middle classes which rose as a corollary to big business under capitalism. No attempt to bring back the original equality of the masses from which the revolution started can be successful. The real power, the real security, the real fruits of the revolution, fall to the new privileged bureaucracy, even if for some short time the thesis that all shall receive according to the quantity of work they render finds spectacular expression in a stunt like that of Russian Stakhanovism.

The failure of the socialist revolution in the precapitalist countries—the only ones where it is still possible and can still appeal to the masses—was admitted by the Russians themselves when they "postponed indefinitely" the day when the true socialist state of freedom would be realized. This—translated from Marxist into ordinary terms—means that the time will never come when the minority which has seized the power in the name of the proletariat will hand this power over to the proletarian masses. The dictatorship can no longer be justified as one of the proletariat over the bourgeois enemies, with those enemies completely destroyed. It is therefore obvious that it is a dictatorship over an unequal and unfree proletariat itself. Stalinism is indeed not socialism. But this is not, as the communist opposition maintains, on account of some sinister conspiracy. It is simply because the actual inevitable consequences of the socialist revolution make socialism impossible.

These matters take up an unwarranted amount of space in our contemporary intellectual discussion. In reality they have no influence at all upon developments in the industrialized countries of central and western Europe and even less upon the United States. In industrialized Europe the belief in socialism as a creed and as the future order had ceased to exist long before it was put to the test in Russia. The process of disintegration was slow and gradual. If there is any specific date at which it can be supposed to have been completed, it was the day on which the World War started. On that day it was shown that the solidarity of interests and of beliefs between the labor movement and the capitalist society of each country is stronger than the international solidarity of the working class. From that day onward the class struggle, though no less real and inevitable, became meaningless and destructive. Socialism had withdrawn its claim to establish the classless society and to be a new order. And on that day Mussolini ceased to be a Marxist. The few pathetic attempts at socialist revolution which flared up in postwar Europe only emphasized the futility and the complete extinction of the creed that had once gripped the masses so deeply. The only remaining alternative to the road that led from the British general strike of 1926 to Ramsay MacDonald's entry into a Conservative government is that which the Viennese workers took, starting with their pathetic attempt to socialize Austrian economics in 1919 up to their heroic last stand in 1934 and to their death in everlasting honor—but in vain—for a free and equal Austria.

Since socialism cannot provide belief in a future social order, the masses are thrown back upon belief in the present order of capitalism, lest modern society should lose all meaning for them. Even the allegiance to the trade-union socialism, which now remains as the sole residue of the old creed of revolutionary socialism, is entirely dependent upon the belief in the validity and rationality of the capitalist order.

That capitalism is doomed seems to be a commonplace, and it is correct—certainly as far as Europe is concerned. However, the arguments usually put forth in support of this statement—namely, that capitalism has failed as an economic system—not only betray profound ignorance of the nature of this system, but are provably wrong. As an economic system that produces ever-increasing quantities of goods at ever-decreasing prices and with steadily shorter hours of labor, capitalism has not only not failed, it has succeeded beyond the wildest dreams. There is no economic reason why its greatest successes should not be just ahead in the industrialization of the colonial countries and in the industrialization of agriculture.

As far as the potential economic future of the capitalist system is concerned, Henry Ford—that grand old man of modern capitalism who embodies all that is best and all that is worst in mass-production monopoly capitalism—is undoubtedly right, and the professional grave-diggers of capitalism wrong. But Ford, no less than his critics, forgets that economic expansion and increase are not aims in themselves. They make sense only as means to a social end. They are highly desirable as long as they promise to attain this end. But if this promise is proved illusory the means become of very doubtful value.

Capitalism as a social order and as a creed is the expression of the belief in economic progress as leading toward the freedom and equality of the individual in the free and equal society. Marxism expects this society to result from the abolition of private profit. Capitalism expects the free and equal society to result from the enthronement of private profit as supreme ruler of social behavior. Capitalism did not, of course, invent the "profit motive"; nor is it sufficient evidence for the Marxist assertion that all past societies were fundamentally capitalist to show that the lust for profits was always a strong motive of individual action. Profit has always been one of the main motivating forces of the individual and will always be—regardless of the social order in which he lives. But the capitalist creed was the first and only social creed which valued the profit motive positively as the means by which the ideal free and equal society would be automatically realized. All previous creeds had regarded the private profit motive as socially destructive, or at least neutral. Their social orders had intentionally subjected the economic activity of the individual to narrow limitations so as to minimize its harmful effects upon the spheres and activities considered socially constructive. At best, they arbitrarily imposed restrictions or gave freedom according to political expediency and as a socially irrelevent matter. To put a positive social value upon the profit motive requires the freeing of individual economic activity from all restrictions. Capitalism has therefore to endow the economic sphere with independence and autonomy, which means that economic activities must not be subjected to noneconomic considerations, but must rank higher. All social energies have to be concentrated upon the promotion of economic ends, because economic progress carries the promise of the social millennium. This is capitalism; and without this social end it has neither sense nor justification nor possibility of existence.

From the height of the material economic comfort which we have achieved as result of one hundred fifty to two hundred years of capitalist progress, we might be inclined at first glance to ridicule the assertion that the economic freedom to which we owe all these achievements may be anything but a good in itself. Yet it did not appear as such even to the worst sufferers from the old precapitalist order, the wretched artisans and the starving serfs. To them economic freedom held only terrors. It asked them to give up their security; though it was a miserable, meaningless security of starving it was the only thing they had. And it promised them nothing economically but insecurity. It took away their small hereditary plots, the tariff protection of their markets, the

minimum prices of the guilds; and it threw them upon
their skill and upon their wits. They accepted this freedom only because it carried the promise of ultimate social and economic equality. Even so, they revolted often
enough against their liberation. There is an unbroken
chain of opposition to the introduction of economic freedom and to the capitalist autonomy of the economic
sphere. This opposition invariably came from the very
classes which ought to have benefited most—witness the
Luddites in England, the Corn revolts of the Irish peasants, the revolt of the Silesian linen weavers, and the un-
rest of the Russian peasantry after the Stolypin reforms
of 1906 which converted the Russian communal village
farms into individual holdings in the name of economic
freedom and economic progress. In every case the opposition could only be overcome—peacefully or by force—
because of the promise of capitalism to establish
equality.

That this promise was an illusion we all know. Economic progress does not bring equality, not even the
formal equality of "equal opportunity." It brings instead
the new and extremely rigid unequal classes of the petty
bourgeoisie into which it is as difficult to graduate from
the proletariat—at least in Europe—as it is difficult to
rise out of them into the class of entrepreneurs. If the
classes of modern industrial society are not hereditary
by law, they have almost become so in fact. Probably it

was easier in seventeenth- and eighteenth-century society to rise to the top, once one had raised oneself the first step out of the amorphous mass on the bottom, than it is in European twentieth-century society to rise from the class of one's birth into the next higher class.

This failure to establish equality by economic freedom has destroyed the belief in capitalism as a social system in spite of material blessings, not only for the proletariat but among the very middle classes who have benefited most economically and socially. This shows in the tenacity with which the lower middle classes and the upper working classes—the layers hardest hit by inequality—cling to the fallacy that "free competition" among many small units is the most efficient method of industrial production, in spite of the quite obvious fact that integrated mass production is the most efficient and cheapest method, though the most unequal one. Mass production on a large scale might still retain all economic elements of competition; but socially it means complete monopolization. Yet it is only through this belief in "free competition," which implies that any increase in efficiency will increase equality of opportunity and of social status, that the belief in capitalism itself can be maintained. As soon as it is exploded these lower middle classes turn away from capitalism as they did in central Europe. The paramount importance of the promise of equality explains the pathetic struggle of the lower mid-

dle classes to send their children to college and university. They see in the professions—supposedly outside the
sphere of capitalist economy—the channel through which
that equality can be reached which is denied to them and
their children in business life. When the European college graduates realized that this too had been an illusion,
they turned away from capitalism. But the most important, most conclusive proof both of the importance of the
social promise and of the degree to which the faith in it
has been destroyed, lies in the acceptance by the European working class of the Marxist thesis of the "impoverishment of the masses" as gospel truth. That this thesis is
wrong—both as to the absolute economic status of the
worker and as to the discrepancy between his status and
that of the propertied classes—has not shaken belief in
it at all and is really quite irrelevant. For the thesis intends nothing but that the worker should feel that he is
becoming more and more unequal and that he has less
and less chance to rise out of the ranks of the proletariat.
It is highly significant that he formulates this correct impression in a statement which pronounces capitalism a
failure.

To state exactly when the belief in capitalism was
finally disproved is, of course, impossible. But it was
reduced to absurdity on the day when Henry Ford
showed the world that mass production is the cheapest
and most efficient form of production. Since then eco-

nomic progress necessarily has involved greater inequality. The European belief in capitalism as a social order would, however, have collapsed much earlier but for two factors. One—probably a minor one—was the economic imperialism of the nineteenth century which provided oversea outlets and pickings for the middle classes. The other and decisive factor was the existence of the United States.

The earlier influences which the United States had upon the victory of capitalism and formal democracy in Europe—the influence of the Declaration of Independence and of the Constitution upon the French Revolution; the influence of Jeffersonian democracy upon the transformation of the Whigs into Liberals in England and upon the Nonconformist conscience; the direct influence of Hamilton upon Bismarck's Germany—probably cannot be exaggerated. But they pale compared to the intangible and indirect support to capitalism which began in the second half of the century. To the European masses who slowly realized that their dream of equality through economic freedom had been shattered, the existence of the truly equal, truly free, truly democratic country of "unlimited possibilities" became proof that their creed was the right one in spite of their disillusionment at home. The "success story" of the poor newspaper boy who became a millionaire, of the boy from the log cabin who became President, were their sagas and legends even more than they were the sagas of the American masses. The most illiterate peasant in the Balkans who did not even know the name of his county-seat knew about America, about its free land and its absence of landlords. This importance of the United States both as safety valve and as living example for European capitalism shows graphically in the changes in the racial and geographical origin of the immigrants to America during the nineteenth century, which followed precisely the progress of capitalism from west to east throughout Europe. First came the English and Scots of the Industrial Revolution; then, simultaneously with their "liberation" from feudal security, the Irish; the Germans after the collapse of the equalitarian dream in 1848; later, Scandinavians, Czechs, Italians, Hungarians; after 1880, when Russia began to industrialize her western provinces, the Jews, Poles, Lithuanians, Finns; finally, simultaneously with the penetration of the decadent Turkish empire by the democratic and capitalist ideas of the "Young Turks," the people of the eastern Mediterranean. They all came to America because they had been deprived of their meager security in the name of equality and then cheated out of their equality by the actual development of capitalism. They all came to America because it offered actual equality.

The importance of America as an ideological mainstay of European capitalism reached its peak immediately after the World War. Then the hope of attaining equality through the adoption of American political and economical methods prevented social collapse even in the defeated countries. Although this hope was not realized, America did maintain Europe's social fabric by the loans she poured out during the twenties. The American collapse of 1929 was, therefore, an even greater shock to the European belief in capitalism than to that of Americans themselves. But the magic power of America as the land of equality still lingers. It shows itself in the anxiety of the dictators to portray the United States as a country of violent class wars and rank oppression of the lower classes as well as in the eager attention with which the European masses have been following the New Deal. Yet by now the disintegration of the European belief in capitalism has proceeded too far to be checked by anything. It has been proved beyond possibility of mistake and beyond appeal that capitalism cannot create equality. Economic success, prosperity, and material progress may conceal for some very limited time the extent of this collapse of the capitalist creed; but they will not be able to restore it or even to delay the consequences materially.

Capitalism has been proved a false god because it leads inevitably to class war among rigidly defined classes. Socialism has been proved false because it has been demonstrated that it cannot abolish these classes. The class society of the capitalist reality is irreconcilable with the capitalist ideology, which therefore ceases to make sense. The Marxist class war, on the other hand, while it recognizes and explains the actual reality, ceases to have any meaning because it leads nowhere. Both creeds and orders failed because their concept of the automatic consequences of the exercise of economic freedom by the individual was false.

This failure has the most direct repercussions in the economic sphere. It makes senseless or at least doubtful every institution in political life. But its most profound effect is on the fundamental concept on which all society is founded: the concept which man has of his own nature and of his function and place in society. The proof that the economic freedom of the individual does not automatically or dialectically lead to equality, has destroyed the very concept of the nature of man on which both capitalism and socialism were based: Economic Man.

Every organized society is built upon a concept of the nature of man and of his function and place in society. Whatever its truth as a picture of human nature, this concept always gives a true picture of the nature of the society which recognizes and identifies itself with it. It symbolizes the fundamental tenets and beliefs of society by showing the sphere of human activity which it regards as socially decisive and supreme. The concept of man as an "economic animal" is the true symbol of the

societies of bourgeois capitalism and of Marxist socialism, which see in the free exercise of man's economic
activity the means toward the realization of their aims.
Economic satisfactions alone appear socially important
and relevant. Economic positions, economic privileges,
and economic rights are those for which man works. For
these he wages war, and for these he is prepared to die.
All others seem mere hypocrisy, snobbism, or romantic
nonsense.

This concept of Economic Man found its first literary
expression in the *homo œconomicus* of Adam Smith and
his school. He was their all-cunning and completely unscrupulous fictional character, who not only always
wanted to act according to his best economic interests,
but also always knew how to do so. This abstraction,
though useful in a textbook, was, of course, too crude and
too much of a caricature to be accepted as a real definition of man's true nature. Even bourgeois capitalism
adopted Marx's refined and corrected edition of the Economic Man who, in the last analysis, will tend to act according to his "class interests," even if he neither wants
to do it nor knows that he does it.

The outward sign of the emergence of the concept of
Economic Man as the basis of society was the emergence
of economics as a science. As soon as the concept of
Economic Man had been accepted as representing the
true nature of man, the development of a science of eco-

nomics became not only possible but imperative and essential.

Economics as a social or "moral" science dealing with the social behavior of man and with institutions devised by him, can only claim to be a science if the economic sphere is regarded as autonomous, if not as supreme, and economic aims as desirable over and above all others. Otherwise economics can offer only a historical or classifying description or technical rules for realizing certain economic intentions. But it can supply no "laws" of economic cause and effect—the criterion of a science. While in the truly empirical natural sciences it is the rule that counts, it is the exception which is decisive in all social sciences, owing to their fundamentally dogmatic and unempirical character. The dependence of the science of economics on the concept of Economic Man is greatly enhanced by this fact. A zoologist is entitled to disregard the atypical behavior of a single rabbit which fails to shed its fur at the normal time. But the whole scientific system of classical economics collapsed when Henry Ford started out to obtain a monopoly by cheaper prices and larger production in blissful ignorance of the "economic law" according to which monopolies reduce production and raise prices.

The degree to which actual developments comply with the laws of economic science unfailingly indicates, therefore, the degree to which the economic sphere is actually regarded as supreme and to which the society based upon Economic Man is accepted as valid and purposeful. At first glance it might appear that the science of economics has never been more dominant than just now and that, therefore, the belief in the society of Economic Man could never have been stronger. Nation after nation has entrusted the management of its affairs to the trained economist. He is in demand as business executive and as political leader, as lecturer and as radio commentator. But this superficial appearance is deceptive. We have installed the economist in a last desperate effort to save the society of Economic Man, just as the eighteenth century installed the philosopher—the rationalist, "enlightened," historically trained scholar—on its shaky thrones. And like the Philosopher-King in the eighteenth century, the Economist-Prime Minister in the twentieth has failed.

Although the professional economist seems to have the power, actual developments have been taking a course which all economists—however much they differ among themselves—had declared to be "impossible." We were told that the gold standard could never be abandoned by the very men who did it. Dr. Schacht, father of bilateral trade agreements, owes his reputation as a professional economist largely to his learned and conclusive exposition that such agreements cannot possibly work. That Russia must break down "within the next six months" has been believed by capitalist and socialist economists alike for the last twenty years. And that neither in Germany nor in the United States is there as yet price inflation, appears as "impossible" to the economist as the miracles of the early church to the modern physicist and biologist. This can only mean that the teachings of economic science have ceased to correspond to social reality.

It is not that the standard of knowledge of the economists has deteriorated. It is the belief in the desirability and in the necessity of the sovereignty and autonomy of the economic sphere that is disappearing; and with the belief, the reality. The masses have realized that the exercise of free economic activity will not and cannot lead to the establishment of the free and equal society. They therefore refuse to regard economic behavior as "typical" and socially desirable behavior. They refuse to accept institutions simply because they serve economic ends, satisfactions simply because they are economic satisfactions. From the point of view of the economist all this is impossible. He cannot explain how it could happen. Economic penalties may be very severe following the disregard of such economic laws as are not technical rules but real natural laws translated from the realm of physics or geology into economic language, like the law of diminishing returns. Even so, the masses are willing to pay penalties. That the threat of such penalties does not deter the European masses shows that the objectives which they hope to attain through the disregard of economic laws appear to them more important than economic objectives. For them, the economic has ceased to be the autonomous and sovereign sphere to which all the others must be subordinated.

The collapse of the society of Economic Man was inevitable as soon as Marxism had proved itself unable to realize the free and equal society. Beyond Marxism there is no possibility of reconciling the supremacy of the economic sphere with the belief in freedom and equality as the true aims of society. And the only justification, the only basis for Economic Man or for any society based thereon, is the promise of the realization of freedom and equality.

It is the very essence of Europe that it conceives man as free and equal. That these basic conceptions were already latent in the Greek City-State and in the Roman Empire, explains our feeling of proximity to those eras —a feeling which we do not have for contemporary South America, for example. With Christianity, freedom and equality became the two basic concepts of Europe; they are themselves Europe. For two thousand years all orders and creeds of Europe developed out of the Christian order and had freedom and equality as their goal and the promise of the eventual attainment of freedom and equality as their justification. European history is the history of the projection of these concepts into the reality of social existence.

Realization of freedom and equality was first sought in the spiritual sphere. The creed that all men are equal in the world beyond and free to decide their fate in the other world by their actions and thoughts in this one, which, accordingly, is but a preparation for the real life, may have been only an attempt to keep the masses down, as the eighteenth century and the Marxists assert. But to the people in the eleventh or in the thirteenth century the promise was real. That every Last Judgment at a church door shows popes, bishops, and kings in damnation was not just the romantic fancy of a rebellious stonemason. It was a real and truthful expression of that epoch of our history which projected freedom and equality into the spiritual sphere. It saw and understood man as Spiritual Man, and his place in the world and in society as a place in a spiritual order. And it made theology an "exact science."

When this order collapsed, freedom and equality became projected into the intellectual sphere. The Lutheran creed, which made man decide his fate by the use of his free and equal intellect in interpreting the Scriptures, is the supreme—though neither the only nor the last—metamorphosis of the order of Intellectual Man. After its breakdown freedom and equality became pro-

jected into the social sphere: man became first Political
and then Economic Man. Freedom and equality became
social and economic freedom and social and economic
equality. Man's nature became a function of his place in
the social and economic order in which his existence
found its explanation and its reason.

In Marxism this conception of the world and of society reaches its climax. The faith in the attainability of
freedom and equality in and through the economic
sphere is restated and based upon the very failure of
capitalism to reach this goal. Marx derived the promise
of the attainment of the classless society from the reality
of class war, which proved the failure of the attempt to
attain equality through harmony in the economic sphere.
The failure of democracy to be anything but formal—
i.e., unequal—"proved" the imminence of the truly free
society. The impoverishment of the masses—i.e., their
growing inequality—becomes the vehicle to obtain
equality and wealth. That all history is the history of
class wars proves that all history leads to the classless
society.

This is one of the most grandiose, most profound
creeds which Europe has ever produced. As long as the
capitalist order survives it will be its most trenchant
critique. But Marxism hinges on a dialectic play upon
the concept of freedom, which comes dangerously near
abandoning freedom altogether. Marxism, like bourgeois

capitalism, sees in the establishment of true freedom the final aim of society. The opposition to capitalist society stems from this emphasis on freedom. But in order to prove that man will be free in the socialist state, Marx had to deny not only that he is actually free under capitalism, but even that he has the faculty of being free. The promise of socialism lies in the "automatism" of economic laws which deprive the individual of his freedom of will and make him subject to his class situation, i.e., unfree. It is as bold and daring a piece of speculative theology as the antinomy between actual freedom and complete predestination in Calvinism, to which Marxism bears a striking resemblance intellectually and ideologically and in its historical function.

To the subordination of freedom Marxism owes its tremendous religious force. It gave the creed its inevitability, its certainty of final success, and its entrancing intellectual finality. Without it the demand to believe that the classless society would come because society had always been a society of class wars, or that the greatest inequality would bring real equality, would have appeared nonsensical—and not only in a "rational" age. But Marxism owes to it also its dogmatic and inflexible nature. Its intellectual tension is so severe that the whole edifice threatens to collapse if one stone is touched. Nothing can be changed in Marxism without abandoning freedom as a goal or the promise of its attainment. This explains the extreme vulnerability of the belief in Marxism and the rapidity with which it disintegrated, once the first doubts of the attainability of the free and equal socialist society had appeared.

Capitalism as a means toward freedom and equality had been proved illusory in Europe by 1848; yet until yesterday a very substantial minority still believed in it. Socialism, on the other hand, did not attain the status of a major creed until the closing years of the nineteenth century. Less than twenty-five years separate the first great electoral victory of the German workers from their defeat in 1932 when, with half the country behind them, they suffered without protest the bodily expulsion of their legally elected government by the completely impotent pre-Hitler government of von Papen, who was supported neither by the army nor by the police nor by anyone else. And less than twelve months later they accepted with resignation the destruction of all the achievements which they had won in decades of hard struggle.

With the collapse of Marxism as a creed, any society based upon the sovereignty and autonomy of the economic sphere becomes invalid and irrational, because freedom and equality cannot be realized in it and through it. But while the old orders of capitalism and socialism disintegrated beyond revival and beyond possibility of further development, no new order arose. As we have seen above, it is the characteristic feature of our times that no new concept of the nature of man lies ready under the surface to take the place of Economic Man. No new sphere of human activity offers itself for the projection of freedom and equality. While Europe becomes, therefore, unable to explain and to justify its old social orders with and from its old concepts, it has not as yet acquired or developed a new concept from which new valid social values, a new reason for a new order, and an explanation of man's place in it could be derived.

Through the collapse of Economic Man the individual is deprived of his social order, and his world of its rational existence. He can no longer explain or understand his existence as rationally correlated and co-ordinated to the world in which he lives; nor can he co-ordinate the world and the social reality to his existence. The function of the individual in society has become entirely irrational and senseless. Man is isolated within a tremendous machine, the purpose and meaning of which he does not accept and cannot translate into terms of his experience. Society ceases to be a community of individuals bound together by a common purpose, and becomes a chaotic hubbub of purposeless isolated monads.

This disintegration of the rational character of society and of the rational relationship between individual and society is the most revolutionary trait of our times. Outside the Occidental cultural orbit the irrationality of human existence and of human society is the rule; rationalization, if undertaken at all, is restricted to a very small circle such as tribe or family. But Europe—and Europe alone—has successfully attempted the rationalization of the whole cosmos. To have given a rational explanation of the whole world—this one and the one beyond; to have given every individual a definite place in this rational order—be it in a divine plan of salvation or in a man-made classless society—has been the great metaphysical achievement of Christianity which sets Europe apart from all others. Everywhere else demonic forces roam outside the rational order; they can be conjured or placated, but can be neither comprehended nor influenced rationally. They follow no laws but their own. Europe alone banished and destroyed them. Of course, we have the Devil. But the forces of evil are highly rational; no intelligible image of the world would be possible in which they were not included. Even Marxism had to make devils out of the capitalists, although Marx himself tried hard to show that they were not evil but just tools of impartial economic forces. Compared therewith, Satan with hoof, horns, and tail is a triumph of reason over chaos. But while the Devil can claim full citizenship in Europe, neither the wood nymphs of the Greek nor the rain god of the Swahili have any place in our world.

The developments under capitalism and Marxism did

nothing to prepare Europe for a period in which fundamental rationality would be endangered. On the contrary: in the order of Economic Man the rationalization
of the world is driven to a point where everything becomes not only understandable as part of a rational
entity but calculable as part of a mechanical sequence.
Life insurance which converts death, the most awe-
inspiring, most fundamental fact of human existence—
rationalization of which has been the most difficult and
urgent task of all metaphysics—into something calculable and accordingly mechanical, appears the symbolic
invention of this age. The Marxist theory of freedom,
which makes the incalculable and nonmechanical individual human will subject to the mechanical laws of
the "class situation," as well as the philosophies of be-
haviorism and psychoanalysis, which interpret the even
more incalculable reactions of the subconscious mind in
mechanical terms, bring to a climax the mechanization
of the world. They almost burst the rational order.
Science—the proudest child of this order—has already
taken the decisive step toward the destruction of its own
basis of rationality. Whatever the physicists may mean
by their denial of causation and its replacement by
Chance, they imply that they have reached and even
overstepped the limits of a mechanical conception of the
world. In the same way in which the physicists cannot
find a new rational substitute for their mechanically

conceived law of causation, society has not found a new rational basis to replace the mechanical rationalization of the world which disappears with the collapsing belief in capitalism and Marxist socialism.

The destruction of the order in which the individual has a rational place and a rational function necessarily invalidates also the old order of values, which was a rational order of rational values. Freedom and equality, the two cornerstones of this order, are values which are intelligible and endowed with meaning only as applied to a rational society. Can they have any meaning to the bewildered, isolated individual in a society that has itself lost all rational meaning? And how does the individual react, how is he affected by this destruction of his own rational existence?

CHAPTER THREE

THE RETURN OF THE DEMONS

THE collapse of the belief in the capitalist and socialist creeds was translated into terms of individual experience by the World War and the great depression. These catastrophes broke through the everyday routine which makes men accept existing forms, institutions, and tenets as unalterable natural laws. They suddenly exposed the vacuum behind the façade of society. The European masses realized for the first time that existence in this society is governed not by rational and sensible, but by blind, irrational, and demonic forces.

Modern war appeared to be the denial of all tenets on which the mechanical and rational conception of society is based. This was not because war is amechanical and arational, but because it reduces mechanization and rationalization to absurdity. The machine and the rational, strategical, or economic calculation to which men are just so many impersonal units become autonomous forces of their own. They appear as entirely independent of the control or understanding of the subjugated individual, and therefore as entirely irrational. In terms of human experience the war showed the individual suddenly as an isolated, helpless, powerless atom in a world of irrational monsters. The concept of society in which man is an equal and free member and in which his fate depends mainly upon his own merits and his own efforts, proved an illusion. Consciously or subconsciously, we have come to judge all books about the war by the sole standard whether they convey this experience. Not only are we unable to judge, but we do not care how they rate as works of art, as long as they breathe the isolation, the atomization, the nihilism of war. For this and for no other reason Hemingway, Remarque, and Sassoon found immediate response. The only writer of first rank in the postwar period who accepted war not only as inevitable but as an essential sphere of human life was the German Ernst Juenger. It is highly significant that he also accepted the isolation and atomization of the individual and attempted to find a new concept of man—without individual function or justification, almost without individual existence.

The great depression proved that irrational and incalculable forces also rule peacetime society: the threats of sudden permanent unemployment, of being thrown on the industrial scrap heap in one's prime or even before one has started to work. Against these forces the individual finds himself as helpless, isolated, and atomized as against the forces of machine war. He cannot determine when unemployment is going to hit and why; he cannot fight it, he cannot even dodge it. Like the forces of war, the forces of depression reduce man's rational and mechanical concept of his own existence to absurdity, because they are the ultimate consequences of his rational and mechanical society. And like the forces of war, depression shows man as a senseless cog in a senselessly whirling machine which is beyond human understanding and which has ceased to serve any purpose but its own.

These experiences are not due to anything inherent in the character of war and depression as such. They are exclusively due to the disintegration of the belief in the foundations of our society. It becomes impossible to coordinate the rational existence of the individual to a society which breeds wars and depressions. As far as modern war is concerned, it will, of course, always be regarded as a terrible evil. But that it appears irrational and senseless is not a necessary consequence. To both sides in the civil war in Spain modern warfare appears rational in spite of its terror. The World War came to appear senseless and chaotic only because it revealed the main foundation of the social order as illusory. Otherwise the war would have made sense as part of this rational order. The sacrifices of the individual would have appeared as a major tribute to the order and as the highest confirmation of its fundamental truth, in the same spirit in which they were regarded by the soldiers of the French Revolution or by the Prussian and Austrian volunteers who rose against Napoleon in 1813.

The World War itself made sense as long as the belief persisted that it was fought "to make the world safe for democracy." The hope that victory would lead to the final and definite establishment of the reign of liberty, progress, equality, prosperity, and of all the other tenets of the rational order of capitalism, kept the masses in the trenches. It brought the United States into the war as an ally of the Powers fighting for democracy, and thus ensured their victory; whereas, according to all precedents, America should have fought—if at all—against England, who had abolished the historical "freedom of the seas." The conviction that they fought against the creed in which they themselves believed, literally defeated the Germans. It broke the Austrian army almost before the war had started. It led to the virtual resignation of the German civilian authorities, who could not wage war against the tenets of democracy with moral authority—although they knew well from the history of their own country that modern wars can be won only under civilian command, they had to abdicate to the military. A direct consequence was the fatal mistake of the peace of Brest-Litovsk which kept one-and-a-half million German soldiers in the East just at the time when their use in the West might have brought speedy victory before the arrival of the Americans, and in all probability might have prevented the complete military collapse. The civilian leaders of the German people foresaw all this: but had they pleaded for a sensible and speedy peace with Russia, they would have been pleading the cause of democracy and socialism—that is of Germany's enemies. How conscious the German people themselves were of the situation is shown by the agreement of all their serious political thinkers—liberals like Walther Rathenau no less than extreme nationalists like Moeller van den Bruck or Juenger—that a German victory was impossible because it would have been a "perversion of history." And the pathetic enthusiasm with which Wilson's Fourteen Points were greeted by the people on both sides shows the profundity of the belief that the war had served a desirable rational purpose.

It is still widely held that the peace could have realized the principles for which the war had been fought but for the folly of Versailles, the aftermath of French hegemony in Europe, or the abstention of the United States from the League of Nations. Actually, however, it is more than improbable that any action on the part of the United States would have influenced fundamentally the course of postwar Europe. Nor could the peace treaties and the years afterwards have been very different. The war was necessarily fought in the name of democracy, freedom, international economic co-operation, self-determination, and all the other tenets of liberal capitalism. But its reality was by equal necessity a fight for imperialist hegemony which could not have ended otherwise than by a peace of inequality and by the very negation of all the tenets of equal and free society.

For the reality of industrial society is one of inequality. The failure to realize the ideals for which the war had been fought is directly due to the basic and fundamental cleavage between the ideals and concepts of the society of Economic Man and its actual structure revealed by the war. This disparity alone destroyed our belief in the democratic creed. New terms such as "have-not" versus "have" nations—by which we project the ideology of class war into international relations—are a complete rejection of the formal equality of bourgeois liberalism, as well as a denial of the international solidarity of classes found in Marxism. This disparity shows itself also in the identification of the idea of democracy with the reality of the territorial order established at Versailles. It became impossible on the one hand to change the frontiers without abandoning democracy. On the other hand, the masses refused, in the case of Czechoslovakia, to fight for democracy, since that would have meant fighting for Versailles.

The irrationality of the depression is even more owing to a change in our beliefs. Up to 1929 depression was regarded not only as entirely rational but almost as desirable—or at least as necessary. Its sacrifices and sufferings were the price of economic progress toward ever-greater economic achievement and the realization of the free and equal society of Economic Man, either through the economic harmony of capitalism or through the dialectic automatism of Marxism. Unemployment and misery, lower wages and bankruptcies, were "nature's medicine" for the growing economic and social body. This view made the great depressions of the 1830's and of 1873 seem not only tolerable but rational, sensible, and salutary; although, as economists and politicians never tire of pointing out, both were more severe than the great depression of 1929.

At the onset of the depression this traditional view of the function of the trade cycle was still deeply ingrained in the automatic routine mentality. It disappeared almost overnight in all European countries when the routine was broken by the crisis. This shows that the people are no longer willing to make sacrifices for the sake of economic progress, that they do not consider economic progress worth the price. Economic progress no longer appears to them as the supreme means to a supreme goal. The monetary theories of the business cycle—such as those of Keynes, Irving Fisher, or Major Douglas—by denying the necessity and the salutary effects of depression, deny that depressions are rational parts of a rational order. It is highly significant that these theories did not become widely accepted or even widely known until late in the twenties; then they captured like wildfire the imagination of masses and leaders alike.

For the common man it is completely irrelevant whether the irrationality of war and depression is owing to changes in their character or to changes in his own beliefs. The individual does not care whether the forces which govern society have become irrational or whether it is the breakdown of his own rational concept of society which deprives them of their rational explanation and their rational function. The fact that the world has no order and follows no laws is all that is important to him. For the last hundred years economists have unsuccessfully tried to discover the causes of the business cycle. The best of them always knew that they could not do much more than understand the last depression. And that there are only losers in war has been a commonplace for time untold. But the individual is not concerned with historical "proofs," demonstrating that the world has not changed. All he need understand is that the attempt to comprise the universe in a mechanically rational order, in which life and death could be understood in terms of a calculable, logical sequence, has resulted in the *return of the demons* as the real masters of his destiny.

These new demons—poison gas and bombs from the

air, permanent unemployment, and "too old at forty"—
are all the more terrible because they are man-made. The
demons of old were as natural as their manifestations in
earthquakes or storms. The new demons, though no less
inescapable, are unnatural. They can be released by man
only; but once they have been turned loose, man has no
control over them—less than he had over the tribal gods
of the ancients or over the djinns of the *Arabian Nights*,
who could always be placated by magic, prayer, or
sacrifice. The new demons are far more unbearable than
the old ones ever were. A Kierkegaard, a Dostoevski, an
isolated, consciously lonely poet or philosopher, might
be able to look at them unflinchingly and yet remain
sane. The average individual cannot bear the utter atomization, the unreality and senselessness, the destruction
of all order, of all society, of all rational individual
existence through blind, incalculable, senseless forces
created as result of rationalization and mechanization.

To banish these new demons has become the paramount objective of European society. Its first reaction
was to try this by further development and reform along
the traditional lines of capitalist-socialist principles. The
whole history of postwar Europe prior to the emergence
of Nazism in Germany—and in the Western democracies until the Munich accord—is a pitifully futile and
heart-rending attempt to restore the reason and sanity of
society and of the individual in this way. From President

Wilson's Fourteen Points to the collapse of the idea of collective security in the person of Anthony Eden, from the first draft of the statutes of the League of Nations to the failure of the disarmament conference, the European masses always hoped for the miracle that would eliminate war from democratic society altogether and for all time. If good will, sincere intentions, and legal draftsmanship alone could have outlawed war, we would have succeeded. But the postwar attempt to abolish war by means of the League of Nations, collective security, and collective disarmament had to fail. By projecting the democratic belief in the eventual harmony of conflicting interests from the social into the international sphere, it produced "international" class war. The maintenance of peace proved to be a cloak for the movement to maintain one group in power. The connection between collective security and the Versailles territorial status is as little the result of sinister plottings or shortsighted folly as the Versailles peace itself, which was largely inevitable. Such glaring contradictions as the famous Article XIX of the League covenant, which provides for peaceful territorial revision on the condition that the sacrifices be made voluntarily, or the armament provisions which scrupulously maintained the sovereignty of every individual Power, were not accidents or hypocrisy. They were inherent in the nature of the attempt to banish war in order to save society. Lenin understood this; hence his seemingly contradictory attitude which condemned war as an instrument of capitalist imperialism but equally condemned the League and collective security as instruments to protect capitalist domination against the destructive revolutionary effects of war. That the Communists later on abandoned this position and became the most ardent advocates of collective security shows the extent to which socialism has abdicated as the revolutionary order of the future, and shows also that international class war can no more promote freedom and equality than can internal class war.

Every rigid legal system that tries to maintain an artificial society by outlawing violence, makes the eventual revolutionary break in legal continuity all the more violent. Just so does the vain attempt to outlaw war in order to maintain society increase the imminence of war by threatening to turn every local conflict into a world conflagration. There is no more striking example than the results of the policy that is associated with the name of Anthony Eden. Its concept that by threatening war the actual conflict could be avoided, is in itself a contradiction. Every time this policy should have been brought to the test—against Italy over Ethiopia, against Germany over Austria and Czechoslovakia—it had to be abandoned hurriedly as soon as it became apparent that the prevention of local violence might require the general violence of a world conflict "to end war." It is significant that this policy led finally on the one hand to the emergence of Winston Churchill and, on the other, to the "peace at any price" policy. Both have given up the attempt to abolish war in order to save the equal and free society of democracy.

Churchill is the only statesman in England or, for that matter, in Europe, whose idea of society—that of the eighteenth century—does not base itself upon freedom and equality. He never understood why war has to be banished; he always preached preventive war and rearmament; and he accepted the League of Nations only as an instrument of imperialist hegemony. The "peace at any price" party, on the other hand, is ready to sacrifice all reality of democracy in order to banish the demon of war. Both look upon the attempt to preserve democratic society by outlawing war with the same derision with which we regard the attempt to maintain feudal society through the Holy Alliance after the Napoleonic wars—the one because society does not seem worth preserving, the other because it cannot be preserved. Neither understands that the League of Nations was not based upon hypocrisy, but upon the most profound and most sincere hope for freedom and peace.

The attempts to save the industrial system by abolishing depression show even more clearly than the attempts to abolish war the demonic character of the forces which we want to banish. We search for a formula, a little secret word, a simple mechanism which will suddenly turn chaos into order. This endeavor has produced a faith in purely magical short cuts to Utopia, compared with which the gullible and naïve credulity in miracles of times past appears discerning and critical reasoning. We are convinced today that all the alchemists who pretended to have found the philosophers' stone were charlatans, and that all the princes, philosophers, and scholars who were taken in were just illiterate boors. Just so an amused future will probably hold that the people must have been either fools or knaves who believe firmly today that all our ills can be cured if we only find each day the formula for the right price of gold or if we only increase the velocity of the circulation of money. A similar hope for a miracle inspires the theories that wealth can be created or increased by destroying commodities and reducing production, or by a different distribution of existing wealth. Yet every one of these suggestions and beliefs is not only serious and sincere, but stems from a pathetically rational attempt to find the lever by which the irrationalized and chaotic machinery can again be made to serve the purposes for which it was devised.

The monetary crank of today believes in freedom and liberty. He tries, therefore, to banish by magic rites the demons which destroy the free and rational society. The prevalence of such cure-alls in the United States is a significant indication that belief and trust in freedom and liberty are greater and more sincere than anywhere else. That there is nothing left but the miracle is not a reflection upon the sincere crank or upon the masses who follow him in their search for a way out of the impasse. It is an admission of the impossibility of banishing the demons by development from, and by reform of, the traditional order of Economic Man.

The contradiction inherent in the attempt to maintain a society by abolishing a consequence which follows inevitably from its very premise as depression follows from economic progress, has gradually been realized throughout Europe. With the breakdown of the "popular front" experiment in France, this recognition has become general. Since then the masses are consciously or subconsciously aware that they must choose between abandonment of the traditional society or abandonment of the attempt to banish the demons. The inarticulate feeling among the very victims of the depression—so noticeable, for instance, in Germany about 1932—that recovery would not be at all desirable and that the whole system should rather collapse, is a perfect economic counterpart of the Winston Churchill policy in international affairs. And the "peace at any price" policy is paralleled by the conviction that, regardless of economic costs and consequences, no unemployment must be allowed in the next depression.

Just as Chamberlain has been triumphing over Churchill, the view that the economic demons have to be banished, even if everything else has to be given up, has been triumphing in the economic field. The masses cannot endure a world governed by demonic forces. Everywhere in Europe the beliefs and tenets of the society of Economic Man have come to be judged only by whether they threaten to provoke the demons or promise to avert and to banish them. The tendency to subordinate everything to this new all-important and supreme goal has reversed our whole attitude toward the desirability of economic progress.

Doubt of the blessings of European civilization for the primitive colonial peoples was the first sign of the revolt against economic progress. This doubt appeared long before the depression, even before the war. But not until after the war did this attitude actually impede economic progress in Europe. It prevented the economic achievement which should have followed the war logically and almost inevitably: the industrial and capitalist penetration of the Balkans. For southeastern Europe had been drawn by the war into the orbit of democracy; its peoples had been liberated in the name of liberty and equality. Besides, this was the only region in Europe where rapid industrial development in an untapped market seemed not only possible but necessary. After promising beginnings and in spite of heavy capital investments, the economic development of the Balkans foundered completely on the resistance of all classes. Here was the first indication that progress had lost its old place in the order of values. Instead of the Balkans becoming "European," large parts of Europe proper— western Poland, Austria, Hungary, Slovakia—which before the war had fully accepted economic progress and the democratic order as supreme goods in themselves, were "Balkanized" and disintegrated socially.

Equally important as proof of the surrender of the belief in progress is the resistance to the penetration of agriculture by industrial revolution. Until recently agriculture had only been touched at its outskirts by capitalist economy. It had been drawn into the industrial orbit just sufficiently to suffer from the laws of free capitalist enterprise. But it had not itself accepted these laws. It had furnished the basis for the industrial expansion and had borne a very large share of the necessary sacrifice. Yet it had not participated in the benefits. Agriculture remained in a state similar to that of the handicrafts and of manufacture up to 1815. It had been largely mechanized, but not industrialized, if we understand by industrialization not just the introduction of rational costing and of machines into production, but the conversion of the structure of the product from the simple yet expensive and scarce commodity to the complex, high-grade, mass-produced, and cheap product.

On the farms we still produce mainly the crops which we produced two hundred years ago, still mainly for the same uses, and still mainly by the same processes.

Yet there are definite indications that industrial methods are about to enter agriculture. "Collective farming," which consciously applies the industrial division of labor and the industrial factory organization, is one of these. "Soilless farming," which changes the entire nature of farming, is another. The search for new farm products to serve as bases for new industries is a third. If the industrial revolution in farming should gain momentum we would experience a rapid expansion in the quantity and value of farm products, in the demand for them, and in the number of workers required. And if this expansion should proceed along capitalist lines another century of capitalist progress could be expected. But instead of welcoming the prospect, all governments try hard to protect the farmer against this development. It is only too obvious that progress in agriculture would not lead to a free and equal farming population, but to the same inequality which reigns in industry. Progress without the promise of freedom is no blessing. Without this promise the threat of serious economic dislocation becomes an unmitigated evil.

From such rejections of economic progress in limited fields we have proceeded during the last years to reject progress altogether. Not even lip-service is paid any more to the god of progress. Instead, security—security from depressions, security from unemployment, security from progress—has become the supreme universal goal. If progress impedes security, then progress has to be abandoned. And in the event of a new depression no country in Europe will hesitate to introduce measures which, while forbidding progress and spelling economic retreat and lasting impoverishment, might perhaps banish the demons or at least mitigate their onslaught.

The same subordination of the old beliefs and institutions has been taking place with respect to democracy. The old aims and accomplishments of democracy: protection of dissenting minorities, clarification of issues through free discussion, compromise between equals, do not help in the new task of banishing the demons. The institutions devised to realize these aims have, therefore, become meaningless and unreal. They are no longer good, they are not bad; they are just entirely unimportant and unintelligible to the common man. He is unable to understand that the general franchise and suffrage for women were political issues of the first order only twenty years ago. Optimists might deceive themselves into believing that this apathy is due to mere "technical mistakes." Proportional representation is advertised as a panacea in England, just as the abolition of proportional representation was preached in pre-

Hitler Germany. But the dwindling substance of democracy cannot be salvaged by a mechanical formula. Wherever it is deeply rooted in tradition and in the historical conscience of the people as something for which they have fought and suffered, democracy can still have a strong sentimental attraction. But this appeal collapses as soon as it is confronted with a reality which demands abandonment of democracy as the price for the banishing of the demons.

Finally, the concept of freedom itself has been debased and devalued. It has been proved that economic freedom does not lead to equality. To act according to one's greatest economic advantage—the essence of economic freedom—has lost the social value that was placed upon it. Regardless of whether it is man's true nature to put his economic interests first, the masses have ceased to regard economic behavior as socially beneficial in itself, since it cannot promote equality. Hence, curtailment or abandonment of economic freedom are accepted or even welcomed if thereby the threat of unemployment, the danger of depression, or the risks of economic sacrifices promise to become less imminent.

Though we refute the past, we have been unable to find a new sphere of human activities which could be accepted as supreme and autonomous and in which the realization of freedom could be sought. We have created no new concept of man which would give to new noneconomic reactions and interests the distinction of expressing his real nature, and to freedom in a new, noneconomic sphere, the quality of real freedom. We cannot replace economic rewards and economic satisfactions by noneconomic ones as the supreme goal toward which the exercise of freedom is directed. Whatever freedom is left outside the economic sphere will, therefore, tend toward the achievement of economic ends; or it will at least be thus interpreted. If we decide that we have to abolish or to curtail economic freedom as potentially demon-provoking, the danger is very great that we shall soon feel that all freedom threatens to release the demonic forces. Freedom ceases altogether, therefore, to be autonomous and supreme. Those orthodox economists who see in currency restrictions and collective bargaining the first irretraceable steps on the road to tyranny, are not as ridiculous as they might appear. That they are right does not, however, diminish the necessity for currency restrictions or collective bargaining. It only shows that freedom cannot remain real and valid in a world which is ruled by demonic forces.

The masses, then, have become prepared to abandon freedom if this promises to re-establish the rationality of the world. If freedom is incompatible with equality, they will give up freedom. If it is incompatible with security, they will decide for security. To be free or not has become a secondary question, since the freedom available does not help to banish the demons. Since the "free" society is the one which is threatened by the demons, it seems more than plausible to blame freedom and to expect delivery from despair through the abandonment of freedom.

The form in which Europe has cast away freedom is, however, very peculiar. Not even in Nazi Germany has freedom been denounced as an abstract concept. On the contrary, the less real freedom there is, the more there is talk of the "new freedom." Yet this new freedom is a mere word which covers the exact contradiction of all that Europe ever understood by freedom.

Throughout European history freedom in the last analysis was always the right of the individual. Freedom to choose between good and evil, freedom of conscience, freedom of religious worship, political freedom, and economic freedom—they all have no meaning except as freedom of the individual against the majority and against organized society. The attempt to realize this freedom can be made by giving the individual rights within society: that was the collectivism of the Middle Ages. Or the rights can lie outside society: the individualism of modern society. But liberties were always minority rights. Freedom is by definition and necessity the right of the individual or of a minority to behave differently without being outlawed. In unfree society the dissenter is a criminal; in free society "His Majesty's opposition"—a perfect expression for the concept of political freedom—is a necessary and beneficial part of society and the ruler of tomorrow.

The new freedom which is preached in Europe is, however, the right of the majority against the individual. It was internationally accepted in the Munich agreement which handed over to Germany all territory with a bare German majority. The Czech minority in these districts, even if it amounted to 49.9 per cent of the population, were deprived of all rights and of all freedom. But the unlimited right of the majority is not freedom: it is license. *"L'état c'est moi"* was not a declaration of freedom and liberty. Since the king was the strongest social unit in seventeenth-century France, the declaration of his omnipotence after his victory over the feudal freedom and liberties of nobility, burghers, Protestant Dissenters, and Parliaments, was a declaration of unrestricted license. Louis XIV, however, never pretended to decree freedom when he abolished it. Fascism, on the other hand, announces that it has succeeded in discovering the secret of true freedom, which lies in abolishing all possible substance of freedom.

The same peculiarity can be found in the form in which Europe abolishes the substance of the other articles of faith of the capitalist and socialist orders. Free economic enterprise, the recognition of the profit motive as a socially constructive force, and the autonomy of progress have to be given up when the masses become convinced that they conjure up the demonic forces of depression. Yet the façade of industrial factory management, financing, pricing, calculating, accounting, producing, and distributing has to be kept up. This is called "true capitalism" or "true socialism." In the political field, individual political freedom, the rights of the socially weaker groups—i.e., of the minorities—the belief in the wisdom of the *"volonté générale,"* in the sovereignty of the people and in the principles of popular representation—all have lost their validity and are being abandoned. Yet the forms of formal democracy—the fiction of the popular mandate, the registration of popular opinion and of the popular will by vote, the formal equality of every voter—are being maintained. Hitler and Mussolini both proclaim that they have realized the only "true democracy," as their governments express the wishes of 99 per cent of the people. Yet by making it a criminal offense to vote against them, both have openly given up the pretense that anybody has freedom to vote. Anyhow, both proclaim that they rule not by popular but by divine mandate.

This is a most important and unprecedented characteristic of our time. The mere façade of slogans and forms is being maintained as an empty shell while the whole structure has to be abandoned. The more intolerable the substance of the industrial order becomes for the masses, the more necessary does it become to retain its outward forms.

In this contradiction is the true cause of fascism. It stems from the basic experience of the epoch in which we live: the absence of a new creed and of a new order. The old order has ceased to have validity and reality, and its world has therefore become irrational and demonic. But there has emerged no new order which would have brought a new basis of belief, and from which we could develop new forms and new institutions to organize social reality so as to enable us to attain a new supreme goal. We cannot maintain the substance of our old order, since it brings spiritual chaos, which the masses cannot bear. But neither can we abandon the old forms and institutions, as this would bring social and economic chaos, which is equally unbearable. To find a way out which gives a new substance, which carries a new rationality, and which makes possible at the same time the maintenance of the old outward forms is the demand of the masses in their despair. And it is this task which fascism sets out to accomplish.

The very nature of this task explains the stress laid upon "legality" and "legal continuity" which has been puzzling so many observers and which has been responsible for the failure to recognize the revolutionary character of the movement. According to all historical experience, a revolution glories in breaking the old façades and in producing new forms, new institutions, and new slogans. But—as discerning observers noticed while the revolution was still in progress—the social substance changes only slowly and often not at all. In fascism the substance of the old order has been ruthlessly destroyed. But the most superficial old form is carefully preserved. No previous revolution would have retained Hindenburg as president of the German Republic while abolishing the republic of which he was the president. This perversion of all historical rule is inevitable in fascism, which has to maintain the forms while destroying the substance.

That fascism opposes and abolishes all freedom, stems by equal necessity from its assignment. Since it is caused by the absence of a new sphere of human activity into which freedom could be projected, the new substance which it attempts to give to society must by necessity be an unfree substance of an unfree society. By equal necessity all freedom must appear hostile to the unfree new goal, the attainment of which depends upon complete compulsion and complete submission. Therefore fascism by its nature must deny all tenets, all concepts, all articles of the faith of Europe, because all of them were built on the concept of freedom. Its own creed must become all the more negative as it becomes the more difficult to save the forms, catchwords, and ornaments of the empty façade of Europe's past.

Finally, the nature of fascism explains why it has to turn against reason and why it is believed against belief. It can accomplish its task through a miracle only. To maintain the very outward forms which provoke the demons and to give a new substance which banishes or rationalizes the same demons, is a contradiction which reason cannot resolve. But it must be solved because the masses can bear the despair of complete senselessness as little as they can bear that of social chaos. They must turn their hopes toward a miracle. In the depths of their despair reason cannot be believed, truth must be false, and lies must be truth. "Higher bread prices," "lower bread prices," "unchanged bread prices" have all failed. The only hope lies in a kind of bread price which is none of these, which nobody has ever seen before, and which belies the evidence of one's reason.

It is not in spite of its being contrary to reason and in spite of its rejecting everything of the past without exception, but because of it, that the masses flocked to fascism and Nazism and that they abandoned themselves to Mussolini and Hitler. The sorcerer is a sorcerer because he does supernatural things in a supernatural way unknown to all reasonable tradition and contrary to all laws of logic. And it is a sorcerer able to work powerful miracles that the masses in Europe demand and need to allay their intolerable terror of a world which the demons have reconquered.

CHAPTER FOUR

THE FAILURE OF THE CHRISTIAN CHURCHES

IT should have been expected that the churches and the forces of religion would have dominated an analysis of modern society. For the churches are the only independent social body to which people of all classes owe allegiance, and which is not built upon the economic as the constitutive element of its rewards, ranks, and distinctions.

One may dislike the importance of the churches and fight against it; or one may hope and work for an increase in their influence. But once the masses had experienced the collapse of the economic concept of society which prevailed in capitalism and Marxist socialism, religion and the churches should have become predestined to fill the vacuum. At least they should have been a stopgap until a new concept of society and of the nature of man could have been evolved on the basis of the projection of freedom and equality into a new sphere. The Christian revival has been expected by many— and by no means only by the perennially hopeful editors of parish magazines.

Most of these expectations were based upon the metaphysical need of the individual in his social vacuum. The despair of the masses stems indeed from the horror of a world that has lost its meaning. Christianity and the churches can, however, claim not only to be handy and convenient as temporary bridges between two eras, but also to have prepared a positive new social substance by persistently resisting the concept of Economic Man and by correctly predicting its collapse.

The history of the hundred years before the World War is usually seen as the history of the growth and development of bourgeois capitalism and of its Siamese twin and antagonist, Marxist socialism. Yet it can be also interpreted as the history of the emergence of Christian criticism of the mechanical and economic concept of society, and of the increasing awareness in the churches that, and why, this concept must fail.

Several Catholic historians have lately attempted to rewrite German nineteenth-century history from this point of view. They make out a reasonably convincing case that Marx, Darwin, and Herbert Spencer, in whom the mechanist concept culminated, had their roots really in the eighteenth century; whereas the creative forces of the nineteenth century themselves grew out of the Christian opposition to this concept. Of course, such a view of history violates the actual developments in the economic and social field; but not more than the usual materialist

approach violates the intellectual and spiritual developments. And it is an open question whether the intellectual
and spiritual advance guard of tomorrow or the economic and social consequences of yesterday constitute
the proper subject of history.

Leaving aside these speculations, it is certain that
since the beginning of the nineteenth century the Christian churches have been pointing out with ever-increasing vigor and correctness the inevitable consequences of
the mechanistic concept of society. That capitalism would
necessarily destroy itself by creating class war was argued first by the French Catholic thinkers of the
Restoration period like Bonald, de Maistre, and Lamennais, as well as by exponents of the German Romantic
Movement like Baader, Friedrich Schlegel, and Görres.
That class war would prove futile and could only lead
to even greater inequality and to despair was seen with
prophetic foresight by the German Christian Conservatives of the thirties and forties like Constantin Frantz,
Radowitz, and Stahl. And that the trend would lead to
the self-destruction of civilization in senseless war and
senseless depression was proclaimed by the Spanish
Catholic Donoso Cortes not much later.

In the spiritual sphere the main currents of religious
thought—those of the Oxford Movement, Cardinal Newman, or Kierkegaard—were equally motivated by the
recognition that the foundations of European society

were bound to disintegrate. They saw the danger. They knew that to be Christian one must oppose the one basic concept of their time. Therefore they fought against the complacent official church. Their success in rousing their churches attests the extent to which their fears were shared by their discerning coreligionists. Even in the political field of formal democracy, which expressed so completely the mechanist concept of society as to leave almost no room for groups who did not accept it, "Christian" political parties arose. They were, at least in part, motivated by foreknowledge of where mechanization would lead, and by the desire to arrest this trend.

The liberal and socialist writers of the past century who discussed these movements within the churches have bequeathed to us the belief that religion only "blocked the path of progress." It is, of course, true that the churches sided often enough with feudalism and monarchy, because these too were antimechanist, anticapitalist, and antisocialist. But the new forces within the churches were far more antifeudalist and antimonarchist than even capitalism and socialism. They concentrated upon the development of amechanic principles to give continuity and strength to the fabric of capitalist and socialist society after the collapse of its substance. The popes and bishops, the fashionable court preachers of Queen Victoria and of the Hohenzollerns, the "official" authors of textbooks and programs might have been quite unaware of all that. They might have believed that all the trouble came from the "greed" of the bourgeois, the lack of religion in the working class, and the "atheism" of the Freemasons. They might also have feared public education as dangerous, fire insurance as interfering with divine providence, and inoculation as "mutilation of God's image." In other words, they might have shared to the full the stupidities, weaknesses, prejudices, and vices of their time and of their class.

But these dignitaries were no more representative of real forces than dignitaries usually are. Unseen by them there developed movements within the churches which tended in a completely different direction. These strove to prepare for the time when, after the collapse of the substance of society, the social structure would have to be given a new basis and a new meaning. Instead of fighting the economic and social developments, instead of longing for the good old days, these forces accepted social reality as an accomplished fact. The integration of the structure of industrial society into a nonmechanical order, not the turning back of the wheels towards a predemocratic and precapitalist system, was the task which they set themselves. And this task governed religious life and religious activities in the century before the World War. Not even the full pressure of reaction in the churches could suppress or seriously impede this trend. Lamennais in France, Döllinger in Germany were driven out of the Roman church as suspected "Liberals." Newman was not accepted until the end of his long life. Elisabeth Fry was shunned by polite Anglican society as a "Red," as were Kingsley and Maurice. But Lamennais' ideas remained alive within the church and begot Tocqueville; Döllinger's teachings became the basis of the German Catholic trade-unions out of which grew Dr. Bruening, the last and the best Chancellor of democratic Germany; and the English Guild Socialists carried on the work of Kingsley within the English churches.

The success of these Christian attempts to provide a basis for a new nonmechanist society belies the widespread belief in the ineffectiveness of religion in our time. Actually, the great majority of the institutions of present-day society which make life tolerable for the masses owe their origin to these religious forces, because they are not exclusively built upon the collapsed concept of Economic Man. The "Nonconformist conscience" in England revolted first against the treatment of labor as a commodity. The first factory acts which limited the working hours of women and children were sponsored by the Christian revival which centered around Lord Shaftesbury and which was hotly attacked by the Liberals as "blackest reaction." Social insurance was developed in Germany by a genuinely evangelical movement; the express intention to give the worker a new social status by giving him security against the mechanism of the industrial machine was denounced by the employers as well as by the socialists, who had not yet turned trade-unionist and who regarded social insurance as an attempt to delay the "inevitable collapse of capitalism." Decent working conditions, a living wage, and protection against accidents were first advocated and practiced by Quaker industrialists; to restore the humanity of the worker, to give him an individuality and personality apart from his machinelike existence as a mere number in his class was the driving idea behind their reforms. The concept of "industrial democracy" goes back to Robert Owen, that almost saintly figure of early capitalism, who was also the father of consumers' co-operatives.

Simultaneously the religious forces attempted to prevent the crushing of the small independent between the upper millstone of capitalist industry and the nether millstone of proletarianization. Many of the agricultural producers' and credit co-operatives were founded by the lower clergy—often against the determined opposition of their spiritual superiors and of the political authorities. Protestants and Catholics alike fought against the feudal estates, against the growth of tenant farms, and against the enclosures which robbed independent farmers of their land—issues which neither the bourgeois Liberals nor the Marxists regarded as worth fighting for.

This revolt of the forces of religion against the economic basis of society assisted in freeing the farmer in Ireland as well as in Protestant Prussia, in the Slavonic parts of the former Austria-Hungarian Empire, and in the Scandinavian countries. A similar fight was waged successfully to sustain the independent artisan not only in his economic and social status, but also in his self-respect and in his intellectual and moral independence. It is highly significant that this movement was started by two men in Germany who came from opposite poles of society and who had nothing in common except the conviction that economic and mechanist society was doomed: Bishop von Ketteler, a descendent of the proudest, wealthiest, and most influential family of the aristocracy, and the proletarian Kolping, who came from the dregs of society and who had to fight his way to priesthood through hunger and humiliation.

The more apparent the disintegration of the society of Economic Man became, the more comprehensive and apparently the more successful became the efforts of Christianity to provide society with a new, nonmechanist basis. In the early years of this century the integration of the fabric of society into a new Christian order seemed imminent. An organization like the Salvation Army, or the work of Carl Sonnenschein, the leader, friend, and adviser of thousands of Berlin proletarians of all denominations and of all political convictions, offered the prospect of a Christian regeneration.

In the field of education the activity of the forces of religion was at least as important and even more successful. The whole system of education during the nineteenth and early twentieth centuries has been dominated by the attempt of Christianity to maintain the free personality and the rational existence of the individual by offering the child a nonmechanist and noneconomic concept of man. All modern education in Europe—including even pronouncedly atheist radical schools—is based upon these attempts of the forces of religion to replace Economic Man. Pestalozzi, who reformed education in Switzerland, as well as Arnold "of Rugby," who created the Victorian ideal of the "religious gentleman," were still mainly motivated by the humanism of the German idealist philosophy and by opposition to the dry formalism of the eighteenth century. But they based their reforms upon the Christian concept of man. The really decisive impulses to education came from avowedly social motives. The English Evangelical who started Sunday School, Wichern, the Hamburg Protestant pastor who founded the first modern home for criminal and neglected children, and the Italian monk Don Bosco, who organized the first self-government of children in the Milan slums, wanted to save and to reconstruct a

concept of man that was not entirely utilitarian and economic but Christian and humanist.

All these men, whether they worked in the social or
in the educational field, expected that the churches and
religion would attract a steadily increasing elite. This
expectation proved substantially correct. Of course, right
up to the war Marxism attracted a very large part of
the independents who, by virtue of their ability to think
for themselves and to question the accepted routine,
qualified as intellectual leaders. But at least in the last
quarter of the nineteenth century the elite drawn toward
religion was superior in quality and influence to that
drawn toward Marxism. After the turn of the century
it was even larger in number.

John Stuart Mill was the last independent European
thinker in the elite of liberalism and Marxism. Toward
the close of his life even he was beset by the gravest
doubts regarding the ultimate consequences of the orders
which he had so fervently advocated. The bourgeois-
liberal and Marxist generations after his death did not
produce one single independent and original leader in
the field of social thought. Of the two greatest epigones,
the one, Lenin, however original and great in the field
of action, confined his intellectual activity deliberately
to comments and emendations of the Master. The other,
Georges Sorel, who tried to continue the intellectual
development of the Marxist creed, ended with the nega-

tion of all its articles of faith, with the complete renunciation of free man, and with the apotheosis of autonomous violence.

On the other hand, a very large section of the independent and original social and political philosophers
of the last fifty years reverted to religion. Their religious
experience was founded without exception on the recognition of the inevitable collapse of the capitalist and
socialist orders, which compelled them to search for a
new basis on which to place the social fabric. To take
some arbitrary examples: of four prominent leaders of
European radical Christianity, the Russian Berdiadiev
started as an outstanding Marxist theoretician; the Eng-
lishman Chesterton as a social reformer; the German
Protestant Dr. Barth is still a member of the Socialist
party; and Dr. Bruening was a trade-union secretary. A
further symptom of the primacy of the social task is the
drift toward Roman Catholicism—a striking reversion
from the trend toward Protestantism that had existed up
to 1850 with but few exceptions. Protestantism as the
"less rigid" order appealed to Christian thinking before
the task of Christianity was seen in the social sphere,
for Protestantism is largely neutral toward social life.
Catholicism as the "stricter" order which claims to be
the fountainhead of all human activities attracted religious sentiment in search of a new Christian society.

Two great leaders of this movement have left exten-

sive records of the reasons and of the forces which drew
them toward religion. Dostoevski, who started life as a
convinced French-Revolution liberal with socialist leanings, was shaken out of his beliefs by the terrible experience of his imprisonment, death-sentence, and exile
to Siberia, which showed him the isolation of the individual in the modern demonic world. All his novels
reflect but this one thesis: that only Christian man can
make the modern world rational and sensible and can
endure its reality. Henry Adams, who, though an American, represents so exclusively the European inheritance
in American tradition and thought that he can be taken
as representative of European trends, was drawn toward "Chartres and Mont St. Michel" by the realization
of the demonic nature of the machine in modern society
and by his search for the "full life" in which man could
again live in an united, sensible order. In his case the
foundation on social purpose and not on individual religious sentiment is particularly prominent.

Just as manifest is the social basis in the Danish
writer Kierkegaard, who promises to become as much
the teacher of the European intellectuals of our generation as Nietzsche and Tolstoy were forty years ago. His
"flight to God" stems from the recognition that the individual is but an isolated atom in the modern world.
To make this loneliness tolerable and sensible and to
make possible a continuation of society by giving the

individual a new set of values and a new basis outside of economic society, is the substance of Kierkegaard's philosophy. It is significant that, while he himself fled into the most extreme Protestant position, many of his pupils have found the road to Rome the better way to solve the social problems.

The most telling example of the trend is the development of the one man who started from the same premises but did not find the way to Christianity: Nietzsche. It might seem incongruous to call him as a witness for the Christian elite. But there is no doubt in my mind that his whole work centers in the attempt to avoid the acceptance of Christianity, and that his breakdown was caused in the last instance—whatever its physical causes —by the realization that he had run into a blank wall where the denial of his own rationality and sanity had become the only alternative to Christianity. He started from a liberal humanism that belonged to the eighteenth rather than to the nineteenth century. He abandoned the facile rationalism of this concept when he discovered the demonic in Greek man and therewith in man altogether. To banish these demons he adopted the romantic-bourgeois liberalism of Wagner. When romanticism failed he tried to create a man who needs no society, no beliefs, no ethical standards, and who, therefore, is mightier than all demons: the Superman. But all these constructions were really attempts to deny the necessity of a Christian basis for society and for the concept of man's nature. When the Superman proved a shallow illusion whereof the last works bear evidence in their resignation and fear, the experiment to set up a valid non-Christian concept of man and of society collapsed.

The metaphysical struggle for a new spiritual Christian basis found immediate and profound response in social and political life. I do not refer to the average routine churchgoer who sees in religion a social convention and nothing else. Bavarian or Italian peasant, or English retired colonel, he is but dead weight and inertia. He is a retarding, purely reactionary element which is largely responsible for the strength of reactionary forces within the churches and which obstructs the necessarily revolutionary task of integrating modern society into a Christian basis. The influence of the religious elite was therefore strongest in minority churches such as the Catholics in England and the Protestants in Austria; whereas majority churches like Catholicism in Spain and Italy, or Protestantism in Prussia, were least touched by it. For the same reason a substantial part of the people who have been drawn toward the new Christian movements came out of irreligious and mechanistic surroundings and had to break with former tenets in order to accept Christianity. Perhaps, the most noticeable development of the last twenty years is the drift of "typically bourgeois" or "typically socialist" groups like the intelligentsia, the professions, and the artists toward a Christian basis against all their former beliefs and against the tenets of their class, and at the expense of much internal struggle and external attack. Even those who remain untouched by religious experience, or those who refute it, like Gide, have to take issue with it. To remain disinterested or lukewarm, as before the war, is no longer possible.

Thus the churches and religion are stronger today than for many a century, since they command the allegiance of an independent minority predestined for leadership. Yet the popular impression that religion and the churches are today more impotent than ever before is also only too obviously correct. There have indeed been some slight developments which could be interpreted as showing a trend toward a Christian basis. It might be held significant that the democracies turned to leaders of the religious elite—Don Sturzo in Italy, Dr. Bruening in Germany, Dr. Seipel in Austria—before they went down before fascism. Or it might be argued that a considerable number of Austrian intellectuals and even a small number of Austrian workers turned to Catholicism in the bleak, despairing years of the Schuschnigg regime, though much of this was undoubtedly sheer opportunism. Altogether, however, all this amounts to nothing. The one important fact is that the political and social activities of the forces of religion appear generally either as outright reactionary or as meaningless fancies. The papal encyclicae on social questions might be successfully tried in a country like Portugal, which has none of the problems of modern industrial society which the encyclicae set out to solve. But, applied to an industrial country like Austria, their teachings appeared as pseudoromantic reaction or as nonsensical theorizing, far removed from the hard facts. Equally invalid were proved the ideas and tenets of the Protestant religious socialists in Germany, who were a genuinely revolutionary body and yet appeared to everyone but themselves as a group of reactionary dreamers.

It is not only the masses who see solely that side of the social and political teachings of the churches which is negative, and who overlook the constructive work of the elite. The churches themselves emphasize in every conflict only the negative, reactionary angle. Their conviction of the untenability of mechanist society forces them into opposition to bourgeois liberalism and to socialism. But they are unable to formulate the new constructive concept of society which they pretend to have. Their impotence therefore abets totalitarian fascism, though they should know and actually do know that totalitarianism is far more antireligious and far more opposed to the fundamental beliefs of Christianity than Marxism at its atheistic worst. The history of Austria and of Spain shows this tragic antinomy.

This inability of the churches and of Christianity in general to find a social basis is as painfully visible in the achievements of the Christian leaders as is their desire to find just such a basis. There is, for instance, little doubt that the driving force in Chesterton's Catholicism was the social end and not private religion. Yet the only social ideal which he was able to produce was significantly enough *The Return of Don Quixote*—the most asocial, most isolated figure in all literature, who lives entirely in his own personal imagination and finds so little use for the real world and for society that he ignores them altogether. And so does Chesterton's modern Don Quixote ignore or overlook all social realities—class war, machines, the decay of society—of which the journalist Chesterton was as keenly aware as any other man in the England of his time. Or take Henry Adams: exclusively social and political reflections and the quest for the "unity of life"—i.e., for a rational basis of society, not private religious sentiment or need—motivated his drift toward the church. But he could not find this social solution and could not obtain from religion the community which he had been seeking all his life. He could only derive from it a daydream of the past and a clearer picture of the present—individual values and nothing else.

The conspicuous and remarkable failure of the churches to provide the basis for a new society is obviously not due to the "godless spirit" of our age which is so often deplored from the pulpits. On the contrary, an age in which an elite can turn to the churches must have a very strong urge toward religion. In spite of this need and search, Christianity and the churches have been unable to provide a religious social solution. All they can do today is to give the individual a private haven and refuge in an individual religion. They cannot give a new society and a new community. Personal religious experience may be invaluable to the individual; it may restore his peace, may give him a personal God and a rational understanding of his own function and nature. But it cannot re-create society and cannot make social and community life sensible. Even the most devout Catholic is today in the religious position of an extreme Protestant like Kierkegaard, for whom God was a purely personal, untranslatable, and uncommunicable experience which only emphasized his own isolation and loneliness, and the utter irrationality of society.

Perhaps the clearest and most pathetic example of the social failure of Christianity is that of the brave and valiant leader of the German Confessional Movement, Pastor Niemoeller. None shows better that the quest for a new basis of society is the motive for turning toward Christianity. Niemoeller, who had been a submarine commander during the war, had come out of it as crushed and uprooted as many other men of his age. He searched for a new society first among the socialist and communist workers in the coal mines and then, after disillusionment, among the first radical Nazi groups. Finally he turned toward religion. He found in religion an individual peace and an individual haven, an individual mission and an individual faith. But he did not find in it a lesson for society. He opposes Nazism from the basis of his individual conscience; but, though he wants to, he cannot find any constructive opposition to it on social grounds. He realizes that political and social totalitarianism implies destruction of the freedom of religion as well. Yet he cannot develop any social or political creed that would correspond to his personal religion.

This is a worse failure for any Christian church than even a complete loss of all believers. A church that is only a tiny, persecuted minority in a vast sea of atheists might still be strong and successful if it gave its adherents a real community. It would emerge triumphantly as soon as materialism had revealed itself as hollow. That happened in the French Revolution. It might well happen again in Soviet Russia in a generation or two, since the tiny minorities who preserve and reform their church form a real community. But a Christian church which, though strong in number and quality of believers, cannot give them more than private religion and private satisfaction, ceases to be a church altogether—at least in the sense in which Europe understands the word. It loses its essential quality as the basis of a rational order of the cosmos and admits that Christianity, which has banished or rationalized so many earlier demons, cannot banish or rationalize the demons that beset our society and our times. It fails completely to understand their real nature as irrational forces outside the accepted European system of beliefs, in the same way in which bourgeois liberalism and socialism fail to understand these forces and try to conceive them as part of their own routine pattern—what I have called above the "anti-fascist illusion." The only difference is that the Christian concept judges the new forces exclusively according to whether they are antimechanist and antimaterialist, whereas liberalism and Marxism measure them by the sole standard whether they are "rational" from a mechanist and materialist point of view. Just as liberals and socialists believe against all evidence that the great majority of Italians and Germans are secretly opposed to Mussolini and Hitler—or, at most, that they are "misguided"—the churches believe against all evidence—including that of their own persecution—that Franco is a "Christian soldier," that Hitler and Mussolini are really saving the world from bolshevism—or, at most, that they occasionally "go too far" in revolutionary zeal but must be all right fundamentally since they are antimaterialist and antimechanist.

I know that I am grossly oversimplifying the actual state of affairs. I am fully aware that a large section of the liberals and socialists does not subscribe to the above crude view. Yet it is this view which alone counts because it represents, so to speak, the lowest common denominator. The same holds good for the churches. Even in countries where the Catholic church is in the majority and where therefore all efforts are directed toward maintaining the mere form of Catholicism, a large group fights incessantly against any pro-fascist attitude. In other countries there is open revolt against church politics—both in Protestantism and Catholicism. The Duchess of Atholl and the Bishop of Chichester in England, Georges Bernanos and Mauriac in France, Cardinal Faulhaber, the Protestant Religious Socialists and the Catholic Workers' leaders in Austria, who have all come out sharply against totalitarianism, are not less but more representative of the majority in the churches than the pro-fascists. Yet it is the pro-fascists alone that become effective. For they alone, by refusing to see the true character of fascism and by insisting on judging it on traditional standards, can make sense of it. The Christians who recognize and understand its true character as the greatest foe of all traditional order and as the denial of all we hold valuable and sacred cannot translate their knowledge into an effective program. For they themselves are unable to rationalize and banish the demonic forces which have caused fascism. They are numerous, right, and impotent; the minority is weak and blind, but alone effective—at least up to the present. The more evidence accumulates that fascism is the greatest menace to Christianity, the more stubbornly will this minority close its eyes and cling to its interpretation. And the majority will remain impotent to fight it. For you can only fight if you have an alternative to offer.

This failure of the churches becomes particularly apparent in their efforts to convince themselves that words and concepts in the demon-ruled world still mean the same thing as in their own order; whereas, they actually have acquired an entirely different meaning and substance. "Authority" in fascism means the rule of brute autonomous force. Within the Christian order it means just the contrary: the restraint of force in the interest of its subjects—the heteronomous justification of power. When Hitler and Mussolini set out to "re-establish authority" they intend to crush all freedom and all liberties and to prove that might is right. Yet "authority" always meant the reign of right over might. But the same groups within the churches who reproached liberalism and socialism for misunderstanding authority as the reign of might over right, only see that the fascist concept is opposed to the liberal and socialist criticism of authority. They do not and cannot see that fascism in its concept of authority attacks and denies from without

everything for which Christianity stands, whereas liberalism and socialism criticized authority from within the
Christian concept of values.

Similarly, the socially effective groups within the
churches cannot grasp the new meaning of the term
"property." Their concept of property is that of an inalienable social right which the individual needs to fulfill his social duties and to discharge the social functions on which his claim to social equality rests. This
view is radically and incompatibly opposed to what
property has become in the demon-ruled world: a completely irrational and unreal, yet extremely powerful,
fiction which carries with it only privileges and no duties.
The opposition within the churches themselves predicted
this development and showed that the separation of
property and control and the subjection of all property
to money-economy would pauperize the masses and en-
rich the few. They also realized that the mechanist concept of society which makes the economic status as expressed in money the sole social standard is the cause
of this degeneration of property. Yet the churches are
unable to understand that property today is something
quite different from what they meant by the term. They
cannot, therefore, abandon the "principle of property"
and must force themselves to believe that property today
is only "slightly abused." That, far more than their
stake as landowners, is at the root of their continual

alignment with the same propertied classes whom they so bitterly attack as materialist and mechanist.

The impotence and inadequacy of the forces of religion just at the time when they are most urgently needed is perhaps the most disheartening feature of the European situation today. Yet this failure was unavoidable; for the most radical, most clear-sighted forces within the churches were trying to achieve the impossible. On the one hand they sought to master the radically new situation arising from the break in the continuity of European development—the new invasion of new demons. On the other hand they wanted to effect the new rationalization from the basis of old forms and institutions which in themselves breathe the spirit of the old society for which they were fashioned or to which they have been gradually adapted. The Christian radical conservatives tried to be revolutionary and yet to maintain the allegiance of the broad mass of inert and therefore inherently reactionary churchgoers. They tried to make the church a new force in a new world, and at the same time did not and could not give up the positions held by the church in the fundamental institutions of the old order—its community life, its schools, its politics, its social structure. Consequently, the sincere Christian revolutionary—nonetheless revolutionary and nonetheless sincere because his object is the fundamentally conservative one of preventing the break in historic continuity—

comes at once and everywhere into inevitable conflict with the vested material and immaterial interests of his own church. In this conflict there are but two solutions: the retreat to the socially ineffective position of "personal religion" or the defence of the existing institutions, which is equally ineffective. There is no solution which allows the preservation of the positions in the old society and the simultaneous creation of a new society.

This is no fault of the Christian revolutionaries themselves. It is impossible to be a revolutionary from within an existing order. Yet a Christian cannot act otherwise as long as the forms and institutions of the churches are intact. The Christian new integration can become successful only after the routine of the churches has been destroyed or, in other words, after persecution or social revolution have rendered impossible the maintenance of the outward institutions. History gives ample proof of the truth of this statement. In the two earlier breaks in European historic continuity—in the thirteenth century and at the turn of the sixteenth and seventeenth centuries—religion did not become a constructive social force until after its institutional character had been forcibly changed from the roots upward. Even in the French Revolution—historically speaking a minor disturbance within the uninterrupted trend of European history—it was the French Catholics in exile like Bonald and de Maistre, and not the Catholics who remained in their positions and institutions at home, who laid the foundation for a socially and politically effective new integration.

That the churches and the Christian religion will be persecuted under totalitarianism beyond anything we have seen until now, appears certain. And therein lies the one real possibility that the work of the revolutionary forces within the churches will ultimately bear fruit. If the fatal duality which ties the new integration to the maintenance of the old positions is being severed from outside, the forces of religion will become socially constructive. Till then they will only give an increasing number of independent minds of increasing quality and increasing courage an individual haven and an individual spiritual home. They will be unable to give the masses the rationalization of a new social order. In their social activity the forces of religion will work not unlike those of Marxism. They will remain bitter and trenchant critics of the existing order from within. In this function their social effectiveness will entirely depend on the existence of the order which they criticize. Beyond that they will fail and have already failed.

The masses, who in their despair search for a new rationalization and a new social order to banish the demons and who must have such an order at once because they cannot face the world in the utter isolation of the society-less individual, can obtain their salvation as little from the churches as from socialism. It does not matter to them that Christianity will continue eventually as the basis of Europe, unless Europe disintegrates for good, whereas Marxist socialism as a creed belongs already to yesterday. They are only concerned with to-day, with the actuality and terror of their despair and with the immediate banishing of the demons.

CHAPTER FIVE

THE TOTALITARIAN MIRACLE: ITALY AND GERMANY AS TEST CASES?

THE breakdown of the belief in capitalism and socialism and in the society built upon them is general throughout Europe. So is the necessity to maintain the outward organization of society. Yet totalitarianism, which attempts the miracle of finding a new social substance for the old social shell, has till now been confined to two of the large European Powers: Italy and Germany.

To find out what caused the democratic system to collapse in these two countries is of paramount importance. The validity and correctness of the preceding analysis of the roots of fascism hinges on it. If the Italian and German developments should turn out to have been caused by factors unique to these two countries and absent in the rest of Europe, our analysis, though possibly a correct statement of the European situation, will have failed to give the real causes of fascism.

Our thesis that fascism follows the disintegration of the old orders implies that democracy in western and northern Europe survives not through the strength of its social promise but because it exercises a mass appeal independent of its social substance. The analysis of the causes of the breakdown of democracy in Italy and Germany will, therefore, answer the politically all-important question how much resistance against the deadly poison of fascism there is in western European democracy. It will also indicate to what extent western Europe may be expected to follow the course taken by fascism and Nazism.

It is widely held that the development of Germany and Italy has been caused by traits and forces exclusive to these two countries. Hitler claims that his movement fulfills "the true destiny" of the German people. Mussolini's "fascism is no export product" was at the time meant sincerely. Opinion in the democratic countries is largely inclined to take the same view and to lay the blame for fascism on the national character and the history of the Italian and German people. The continuity in the aims of Italian and German foreign policy, trends in the literature and philosophy of these two countries, and real or fictitious traits of national character are cited in support of this view.

Such explanations sound very convincing and can apparently be fully documented. Yet the old saying that "national character" is the last resort of baffled historians unwilling to admit their inability to explain puzzling events, fully applies to them. The national character of every modern people is so complex, seemingly so contradictory and so largely determined by intangibles, that almost anything can be read into it.

Only one year before Hitler assumed power a distinguished Italian anti-fascist "proved" to me that France would go fascist first, whereas Germany would remain democratic. He based his superficially very impressive thesis upon those "pro-fascist traits" in French history which manifest themselves in the rapacious and entirely destructive wars and in the tyranny of Louis XIV, in the dictatorships of the two Napoleons, in the reactionary sentiment that caused the Dreyfus affair, and in the pro-fascist leanings of the Catholic and royalist opposition. In Germany, on the other hand, he saw—using the popular oversimplification—the gradual ascendancy of "Weimar" over "Potsdam."

Actually it is beyond doubt that developments in Italy and Germany were not caused by the respective national characters. In the first place, the fact that fascism has become a world-revolutionary force shows plainly that causes similar to those effective in Italy and Germany must be present elsewhere. In the second place, while fascism has assumed similar forms in Italy and Germany, no two other nations in Europe are more different in character and history than the Italians and the Germans. Moreover, it is simply not correct that there has been continuity in foreign policy under fascism. The aims of foreign policy are so largely conditioned by geography and history that such continuity is the rule in all revolutions. Yet Italy has already been forced by the inner dynamics of fascist ideology to change altogether the aims and objects of her foreign policy, and Germany is moving in the same direction.

Finally, the attempt to explain the Italian and German developments by "national character" confuses the causes with the effects of historical events in a manner that invalidates the whole argument. It is clearly impossible outside of Italy to use the symbol of the Roman Empire as fascism uses it. Anti-Semitism could not possibly play anywhere in western Europe the vital social role which it plays in Nazism—though, of course, there might well be persecution of the Jews as an imitative by-product, as there is today in Italy. But these are expressions, not causes, of historical developments. To deduce a difference in cause from these differences in form, accounted for by local conditions, is like deducing a fundamental difference in the causes of parliamentary democracy in England and France from the fact that the one retained the king and the other became a republic. Even if fascism and Nazism could be explained as manifestations of the "spirit" of the two nations, what released this mythical spirit at this particular time as a reaction against bourgeois liberalism and socialism? The cause must have been some factor working upon the national character from the outside.

The outside force which is generally made responsible is the war. Certainly there would have been no fascism without the war, which showed up the inner destruction of democratic Europe. But why should it have led to collapse in Italy and Germany and not in France, which suffered far more than Italy and even more than Germany? The answer as far as Italy is concerned is that "she lost the peace." This is patent nonsense. Territorially Italy received proportionally more than any Allied Power; in addition, she was given hegemony in the Adriatic and a very prominent position in the eastern Mediterranean. And as for the internal disorganization which, according to official fascist tradition, revealed the rottenness of Italy's democratic system, it was certainly exceeded by the collapse which showed in the great French mutiny of 1918. Yet French democracy survived and Italian democracy perished. French democracy must obviously have possessed some power of resistance against the effects of the war which Italy lacked.

Even less satisfactory is the argument as applied to Germany. For in Germany—and in Germany alone— did the war result in strengthening the belief in democracy which had emerged victorious over the prewar German system. That Germany did not turn fascist earlier than Italy is only due to her having lost the war. A militant reaction against Versailles was bound to come sooner or later. But if democracy had possessed any force, this reaction would have strengthened the belief in the bourgeois or socialist creed, in "industrial democracy," and in the democratic self-determination of nations. Indeed, all German opponents of Versailles, beginning with Walther Rathenau, predicted this development. Logically it should have run along the same lines as the French *revanche* movement after 1870, which culminated in the radicalism of Clemenceau. Germany actually started in that direction. For years it seemed as if she would assume the leadership in a democratic movement against imperialism.

To answer the question as to what caused democracy to collapse in Italy and Germany we must find which social and political traits common to these two countries are not shared by the rest of Europe. There is one, and only one, such common social characteristic. It can be described in various ways. One might say that in these two countries the bourgeois order was introduced from above and not through revolution from below. Or one might say that while Italy and Germany had democratic institutions and a numerically strong bourgeoisie and proletariat, these classes never obtained control of the substance of government; the "political professor" in Germany and the "political lawyer" in Italy remained socially powerless, even when they were admitted to a seat in the cabinet. Or, finally, Italy, Germany, and the western parts of the old Austro-Hungarian monarchy might be regarded as having formed the eastern fringe of European democracy—a sort of military frontier where democracy's tenure was never quite secure. All these formulations mean one thing: the great experience of the nineteenth century in Italy and Germany which attracted the emotional and sentimental attachment of the masses was not the victory of the bourgeois order but national unification. The revolutionary movements were national primarily and democratic secondarily. The wars were fought and the sacrifices of blood were made for national unity. The bourgeois order was primarily accepted as a means toward national unification. The tenets and slogans of the bourgeois order had no sentimental appeal; their strength lay in their social promise and substance. They had, therefore, no independent emotional and sentimental existence in the allegiance of the masses. As soon as it was realized that the substance had become invalid, they ceased to exist altogether. In England, France, Holland, and in the Scandinavian countries, on the other hand, the experience and tradition living in the minds of the people is that of the struggle for democracy. National unity had been achieved much earlier, and the democratic creed appeared, therefore, as an emotional value in its own right. Belgium is the

only western European country where the attainment of
national unity and independence occupies first place
in national tradition and sentiment as the great achievement of the nineteenth century. And Belgium produced
in the Rexist party the first serious fascist movement in
the West.

In Italian history this situation found its best expression in the ascendancy of Cavour over Garibaldi.
Cavour—cool, realistic and altogether a product of the
enlightened absolutism of the eighteenth century—had
as little real inner attachment to the cause of democracy as Richelieu, a cardinal of the Roman Church, had
to the cause of the German Protestants whom he supported in order to weaken the House of Hapsburg during the Thirty Years' War. Constitutional monarchy,
parliamentary democracy, free suffrage, and free trade
were in Cavour's eyes means to fight the territorial
princes, and little else. The Italian national state is his
creation. But Garibaldi, to whom democracy was a religion and the supreme end in itself, though glorified as
a romantic hero, remained almost as ineffective in the
molding of modern Italy as Robin Hood in that of modern England.

Consequently, in Italy bourgeois democracy and capitalism never became sentimental and emotional values.
Though modern social and economic tasks made
necessary the development of a bourgeois class, the

bourgeoisie did not become the real master. This is evidenced by the low social esteem in which the most typical bourgeois career, business, has been held. Until after the World War Italy gladly left to foreigners from Austria, France, and Germany the most important tasks in business and finance: the industrialization of the northern plains and the building up of large commercial banks and insurance companies.

The tenets, institutions, and beliefs of the bourgeois order were, therefore, only accepted on the strength of their social promise and could only be maintained as long as the promise held good. The counterpart of this weakness was the dogmatism of Italian socialism and syndicalism. Both were unable to make the compromise with capitalist reality which is possible in the West on the basis of the emotional attachment of the people to the tenets and slogans of democracy. Both were, therefore, driven into a rigid, inflexible opposition which not only deprived them of all capacity to comprehend reality, but also made it impossible for their followers to defend democratic freedom in capitalist society. A similar development took place in literature and philosophy, which had no connection with political reality but as "pure thought" remained politically and socially impotent. In consequence, the teachings of the most liberal, most individual, and most idealistic Italian democratic philosopher, Gentile, could be used as a cloak for the anti-individualism, anti-idealism and anti-liberalism of fascist educational policy.

The best proof that the breakdown of democracy was caused by the absence of an emotional attachment to its creed is provided by Mussolini's own experience. Nothing was further from his original intention than to cause a social revolution. His sole aim was to seize personal power and to hold it. Mussolini's own writings during the years up to 1924 show quite clearly that he thought that society was solid, well-founded on beliefs and institutions, and troubled only by superficial disturbances owing to the absence of a firm hand. If he had been asked to draw an historical parallel he probably would have pointed to Richelieu or to Napoleon III as analogies. In such a situation the usurper of power must try above all to make the existing order and institutions of society serve his personal purposes; and he must, therefore, try to maintain them.

This was precisely what Mussolini intended to do. Yet, of all his attempts to maintain the existing institutions and the existing social order as instruments of his personal domination, only one was successful: he maintained the House of Savoy because the monarchy is part of the sentimental and emotional tradition of Italian national unity. All the institutions which were based upon the democratic creed crumbled, notwithstanding his efforts to keep them alive as tools of his domination. As soon as the substance of the democratic creed disintegrated its institutions collapsed, because they had no independent existence in the emotion and the sentiment of the people.

Thus Mussolini found that he could not keep alive the Chamber of Deputies, as Napoleon III had done. He wanted to limit his fight with the church to a fight against the political party of the Italian Catholics, which was dangerous to his personal regime. Instead, he has been drawn into an ideological struggle, the last thing he could have desired. He strenuously tried to maintain a free economy under the economic control of bankers and industrialists. But it collapsed under his attempt to secure political control. The "corporate state" which had been designed purely as a political instrument of personal power, suddenly assumed independent social and economic functions. In foreign politics, finally, he intended to play the traditional game of a second-class Power which aspires to first rank: always to remain the fulcrum on the balance of power. Yet ideology forced him to set himself against the West. This resulted in the loss of all Italian influence in central Europe and in the Balkans, in a new threat to Italian domination over the Adriatic, and in dependence upon a large power which is bound to prove fatal to the personal rule which is Mussolini's main aim. He has been forced to become a revolutionary by default. The collapse of bourgeois society compelled him to invent and to improvise a new structure of society, completely different and even contrary to his own intentions.

The development in Germany closely parallels that in Italy. The tenets of democracy were also used in the first place as means toward a national end—from 1806 onward when the ministers of an absolute king of Prussia introduced sweeping democratic reforms in order to release the national energies which defeated Napoleon, up to Bismarck's compromise with the liberals in order to force another Prussian king to become the first emperor of the newly united Germany. In Germany bourgeois society was even stronger numerically than in Italy, and even more important economically; yet it was even more impotent politically, and its professions even less esteemed socially. German idealist philosophy, acclaimed as the perfection of thought of the liberal and bourgeois era, was even more remote from reality. The socialist opposition was equally dogmatic and unreal. The emotional and sentimental appeal of the slogans and institutions of democracy would therefore have been equally weak except for the strengthening through the war. This enabled Germany to maintain her democratic institutions through the inflation of 1922-3, which showed up in an unforgettable manner the complete irrationality and the demonic character of industrial society. The fight for international equality revealed that the lesson to be drawn from the war should have been not that democracy is superior but that it is a deception. Then the democratic system, which had no independent hold upon popular imagination, collapsed and the disintegration of the substance of the democratic order spread rapidly to the tenets, symbols, and institutions without encountering any resistance in the emotional or sentimental tradition of the routine mind.

The parallel extends even to Hitler himself. Unlike Mussolini, Hitler is a typical revolutionary. His personal asceticism bespeaks as truly the fanatic as Mussolini's boisterousness and boyish pranks show the man who loves power and action for their own sake. But, like Mussolini, Hitler expected to be able to use the existing social and economic order for his own political purposes. What little economics there are in *Mein Kampf* show a profound belief in the blessings of free competition, private initiative, and noninterference by the government, such as would find the approval of the sternest disciple of Adam Smith. He also shared the early-capitalist belief in the economic harmony of all classes. Hence his conviction that business could govern itself through representative bodies, once the octopus of "monopoly" and "finance capitalism" had been removed. I myself have heard him attack Walther Rathenau and his pupils for having advocated a totalitarian economy which—according to the Hitler of 1931—would make the state a servant of its social structure.

Hitler has accordingly resisted economic and social totalitarianism. He alone supported Dr. Schacht against the entire Nazi party. He personally vetoed the contemplated merger of all German banks into one, and he demanded that the shares of banks and industrial companies which the government had to take over during the depression, be resold to the public. It is not his fault that this reprivatization did not change in the least the complete control which the government exercises over these and all other businesses. He too was forced to invent a new society when the people forsook the tenets of an order the substance of which had melted away. Their despair pushed him toward a social revolution which not only threatens to overshadow his political revolution, but which also threatens to force a complete revision of his foreign policy.

The analysis of the Italian and German situation shows conclusively that the causes which led to the collapse of democracy are not confined to these two countries. What is peculiar to them is the absence of the appeal which the tenets, institutions, and slogans of the democratic creed exercise upon the emotions and sentiments of the routine mind in western Europe.

The resistance of democracy in western Europe depends, therefore, entirely upon the emotional and sentimental allegiance of the masses to the façade of democracy. This allegiance gives the façade some sort of independent existence even after the structure behind has broken down. Such resistance of tradition might be very powerful and might ensure the survival of the outward forms for a considerable time. Italian and German history provide a perfect example of how effective it might be over centuries. It was the resistance arising from the emotional and sentimental appeal which the City-State in Italy and the feudal territorialism of the Holy Empire in Germany had upon the masses which delayed national unification in central Europe from the seventeenth century until the nineteenth century.

But this example shows that, however strong such traditional resistance might be, it remains inert and purely negative. Though Italy and Germany resisted unification for three hundred years, their old orders could neither maintain any life and reason nor develop a social organization of their own. They remained mere shells; while they did not enjoy any of the benefits which national unification conferred upon western Europe, they had to accept all the disadvantages and all the worst features of the new order: administrative over-centralization, princely autocracy, a formalistic law, and extravagant and wasteful courts. And above all they became entirely impotent—politically, economically, and ideologically at the mercy of the West. It is significant that Germany and Italy were Europe's battlefields from the Thirty Years' War to Napoleon.

The fact that her democracies depend entirely upon tradition shows that western Europe would be faced with the same actual problems as Germany and Italy, should her resistance collapse. The forms in which the countries of the West could then try to overcome their problems would, of course, be fashioned to a considerable extent by local conditions. Theoretically it might be quite different from the Italian and German attempts at a solution. But the problems would be fundamentally the same; and that alone makes it likely that the attempts to solve them—whatever the differences in detail—would be fundamentally not very different.

As a test case of the aims of totalitarianism and of the performance of its miracle, Germany is more important in our analysis than Italy. Not because she is a Great Power, whereas Italy will remain in the second rank, and not because Germany is the major threat to world peace, but because Nazism is the real totalitarian revolution whereas Italian fascism is just an imitation. This might appear wrong historically. But until the emergence of Nazism, Mussolini had succeeded on the whole in keeping the revolutionary forces within fascism well under control. Nazism, on the other hand, started out as a revolutionary movement. Moreover, Germany presents all the problems of modern industrial society; whereas

Italy was still largely in the stage of early capitalism up to the great depression. Finally, Hitler had to be realistic from the outset, whereas the Italian temperament allowed Mussolini to confine himself for a long while to theatrical gestures and historical stage properties.

In spite of Mussolini's historical priority, Nazism has assumed the leadership in formulating the new society, the new creed, and the new concept of man. Italian fascism has become an increasingly unwilling follower, largely deprived of its power to choose its course. Nazism is the really decisive test case, the success or failure of which will also decide the success or failure of Mussolini's fascism.

CHAPTER SIX

FASCIST NONECONOMIC SOCIETY

THE most fundamental, though least publicized, feature of totalitarianism in Italy and Germany is the attempt to substitute noneconomic for economic satisfactions, rewards, and considerations as the basis for the rank, function, and position of the individual in industrial society.

The noneconomic industrial society constitutes fascism's social miracle, which makes possible and sensible the maintenance of the industrial, and therefore necessarily economically unequal, system of production. This was at the same time the most urgent task, at least in Germany. By 1932 it had become obviously impossible to continue the capitalist system of production. It was equally impossible to replace it by something else. At the height of the depression the Communists, who alone of all parties preached the abolition of the capitalist system—the German Socialists had accepted capitalism for years—polled less than 15 per cent of the votes. Even they were split into a left revolutionary and a right trade-unionist wing. Yet the great majority of the German people, though they had lost their postwar faith in social-ism, equally despaired of the capitalist system. They wanted neither capitalist recovery nor socialist revolu-tion. In their despair they almost hoped for chaos. Above all, they had become highly conscious of the futility of the inevitable but deadlocked war of each class against all others.

Mussolini did not find himself confronted with this problem until 1934, although there had been a "totali-tarian" faction in his party ever since 1925, when the storm over the murder of Matteoti, the leader of the Socialist opposition, almost overthrew the Fascist regime. Since 1934, however, Italy, like Germany, has had to find a formula which maintains the forms and production methods of industrial society while eliminat-ing the economic as its basis.

The answer to several of the most hotly disputed ques-tions regarding the nature and function of fascism fol-lows from the nature of this task.

It becomes clear, in the first place, that it is pointless to ask which class put fascism into power. No single class can have put fascism into power. That a gang of ruthless industrialists backed Hitler and Mussolini is as far from, and as near to, the truth as that the great toiling masses backed them. Both were necessarily supported by a minority of all classes.

Mussolini had more capitalist support than Hitler;

yet for many years he had to fight the most powerful combination of Italian capitalists, headed by Toeplitz of the dominant Banca Commerciale and comprising the large industrial corporations affiliated with that bank.

Hitler had the great majority of industrialists and bankers against him until late in 1932, when his success seemed practically assured. From that time onward it became a matter of prudence to contribute to his funds, in the same way in which industry had contributed to Socialist funds in the early twenties without ever "supporting" the Socialists. But the support of a handful of individually powerful industrialists like Thyssen or Kirdorf, which Hitler enjoyed after 1929, contributed to some extent to his success, though their importance was much smaller than is generally believed, and infinitely smaller than that of the majority of industrialists who opposed Nazism. But the really decisive backing came from sections of the lower middle classes, the farmers, and the working class, who were hardest hit by the demonic nature and by the irrationality of society. As far as the Nazi party is concerned, there is good reason to believe that at least three-quarters of its funds, even after 1930, came from the weekly dues, paid especially by the unemployed and by farmers, and from the entrance fees to the mass meetings from which members of the upper classes were always conspicuously absent.

Secondly, it is a moot question whether totalitarianism is capitalist or socialist. It is, of course, neither. Having found both invalid, fascism seeks a society beyond socialism and capitalism that is not based upon economic considerations. Its only economic interest is to keep the machinery of industrial production in good working order. At whose expense and for whose benefit is a subsidiary question; for economic consequences are entirely incidental to the main social task. The apparent contradiction of simultaneous hostility to the capitalist supremacy of private profit as well as to socialism, is, though muddleheaded, a consistent expression of fascism's genuine intentions. Fascism and Nazism are social revolutions but not socialist; they maintain the industrial system but they are not capitalist.

Mussolini and Hitler, like so many revolutionary leaders before them, probably neither understand the nature of their revolutions nor ever intended to go beyond denouncing the "abuses" of either side. But, as already explained, social necessity forced them to invent new noneconomic satisfactions and distinctions and, finally, to embark upon a social policy which aims at constructing a comprehensive noneconomic society side by side with, and within, an industrial system of production.

The first step in this direction was to offer the underprivileged lower classes some of the noneconomic para-

phernalia of economic privilege. These attempts are
largely organized in the fascist organizations of the
leisure hours of the workers: "Dopo Lavoro" ("after
work") in Italy, "Kraft durch Freude" ("strength
through joy") in Germany. Of course, these compulsory
organizations are primarily designed as means of political control of a potentially dangerous and hostile class.
They are honeycombed with police spies and propa-
gandists, whose duty it is to prevent any meeting of workers except under proper supervision. The attractions
offered by these organizations are intended as bribes for
the workers. But—and this is their important feature—
they do not attempt to offer economic rewards as bribes,
although this is the traditional form which has proved
effective, from the Romans to the communist regime in
Russia. Though economic bribes would probably have
been cheaper financially, the fascist organizations of the
workers' leisure offer, besides propaganda and the usual
program of political and technical education, satisfactions in the form of theater, opera, and concert tickets,
holiday trips to the Alps and to foreign countries, Mediterranean and African cruises in winter, cruises to the
North Cape in summer, etc. In other words, they offer
the typical noneconomic "conspicuous waste" of a leisure
class of economic wealth and privilege. These satisfactions have in themselves no economic value at all, but
they are powerful symbols of social position. They are

intended to suggest a measure of social equality as compensation for continued economic inequality. They are accepted as such by a large part of the working class, especially in Germany where even the most confirmed Marxists regarded cultural satisfactions as something higher, more important, and more valuable than many economic rewards. The leisure-time organizations fulfill, therefore, a definite and highly important function in the solution of the fascist task. They make the existing economic inequality appear far less intolerable than before.

They cannot, however, make it appear purposeful and sensible. They can ease the problem, but they cannot solve it nor spirit it away. For the different classes still have unequal social functions and unequal social standing in the community. This is the reason for the re-emergence of the organic theory of society, which proclaims the social harmony of the economically unequal and warring classes. Of course, the use of a theory that portrays the different classes as equally important and indispensable members of one social organism is one of the oldest devices for the prevention of class war. It was used to dissuade the Roman plebeians from a revolutionary sit-down strike. In substance, however, the organic theory of the Fascists is as radically different from that of the Romans as from that of the nineteenth-century Romantic Movement. The comparison of the body politic to a human body always served to stress the equal economic function and equal economic importance of the various classes in order to justify an existing non-economic social inequality. Fascism, on the other hand, uses the organic theory to create an equality of non-economic social importance, status, and function in order to balance the economic inequality of the classes.

This is all the more striking inasmuch as fascism originally intended to take over unchanged the old theory, as a proof of the actual existence of economic harmony. The economic "estates" into which totalitarian theory divides society were conceived as economic units which should supplement each other in the traditional way. In the political and social reality of the totalitarian states, however, the "estates" have become social units which claim social distinctions, social functions, and social equality of their own, entirely independent of their economic functions, economic contributions, and indispensability. The German "peasant estate" is accorded a unique position as the "biological backbone of the race" which entitles it to complete social equality and even to definite, though one-sided and intangible, social superiority. The peasant occupies this position regardless of the value of his contribution to the national economy; it is frankly admitted that he is an economic liability. But, just because the economic utility of the small farmer is very doubtful and because his economic

existence is threatened by the imminent industrial revolution in agriculture, it is all the more important from a
national point of view to fortify his social position. Not
only is the peasant estate protected by special laws and
continuously extolled in speeches, pageants, and symbolic celebrations, but it is impressively emphasized by
the regulations which require every town-bred boy and
girl to spend a certain time as a worker on a farm under
the command of a farmer. The economic advantage
which the farmer derives from this supply of unpaid
labor as well as from various other economic subsidies is
not inconsiderable; but it is by no means sufficient compensation for the deterioration of his economic status
through compulsory crop control. His social standing,
however, has supposedly become independent of the
economic status. And it is, according to the fascist theory,
the social standing which really determines the position
and function of the peasant in society.

Similar attempts have been made to sever the connection between the social and economic status of the
other classes and to found their social position upon
considerations outside the realm of economics. The social
prominence, indispensability, and equality of the working class is given symbolic expression in the conversion
of the socialist May-Day into a festival of Labor and in
its elevation to the most important holiday of Nazism.
If the peasant is the biological backbone of the nation,

the worker is its spiritual one. He determines the new human concept which fascism strives to develop—the Heroic Man, with his preparedness to sacrifice himself, his self-discipline, his self-abnegation, and his "inner equality"—all independent of his economic status. Just as compulsory agricultural work is the symbol of the social superiority of the peasant over the urban population, the labor service which all adolescents, regardless of their economic position, are compelled to undergo, symbolizes the social superiority of the worker over the propertied classes.

The middle class has been distinguished by still another noneconomic claim to equal and indispensable social position. It has been declared the "standard-bearer of national culture." The "Fuehrer Prinzip," the heroic principle of personal leadership, confirms the class of industrialist entrepreneurs in their social position. This principle also claims to be based upon entirely noneconomic distinctions. The leader does not owe his social function and position to his economic function and wealth. The thesis that a leader must prove his qualifications in the spiritual field and that he must be deprived of his economic position if he fails on this score, is taken absolutely seriously by its inventors—and by many others.

The semimilitary formations, the Fascist Militia, the Storm Troops, and the Elite Guards, the Hitler Youth, and the women's organizations serve the same non-economic ends. The military value of these formations and organizations is extremely dubious. In Germany the idea of using them as auxiliary army corps was given up a long time ago. But to the extent to which the military value of these organizations decreased, their social importance increased. Their purpose is frankly to give the underprivileged classes an important sphere of life in which they command while the economically privileged classes obey. In the Nazi Storm Troops as well as in the Fascist Militia the greatest care is taken to make promotion entirely independent of class distinction. Units are socially mixed. The son of the "boss" or the boss himself is intentionally put under one of the unskilled laborers who has been longer in the party. The same principle is applied in the organizations of children and adolescents. It is rumored in Germany that no rich man's son will be admitted to the "Ordensburgen," the Nazi academies in which the future elite is to be trained, although officially the selection is made according to fitness and reliability alone. A wealthy German industrialist of high standing in the Nazi party and an Italian banker who had backed Mussolini before the March on Rome, told me independently and without knowing each other, that they had decided to send their small sons to a military academy, since otherwise they would certainly suffer from the carefully cultivated social envy and from the studied insults of their commanders and comrades in the compulsory youth organizations.

The use of a military form to give the individual compensation for economic inequality is especially evident in the German women's organizations. As these organizations have no real military purpose, the principle according to which they have to satisfy economic envy can be applied without any restraint. Local branch organizations go obviously even further than headquarters desire, for the high command of the Nazi Women's Bund has repeatedly had to forbid the penalizing of members of the propertied classes solely on account of their economic privileges. Nevertheless there are constant reports that "communist provocateurs" abuse their positions of leadership and confidence in order to persecute wealthy members. In Italy developments have been very similar, although at a much slower rate.

These attempts to satisfy the social envy of all classes and to give to each a definite noneconomic superiority in one sphere, have been far more successful than can be gauged from the point of view of the capitalist or socialist creeds. They have certainly gone a long way toward creating a genuine feeling of social equality among the lower classes. This is stronger in the lower middle class than among the workers with their tradition of class-consciousness. It is more general among women than among men. It is more valued by young people who do not yet have to earn their living than among adults. But it is effective to some extent in all classes, all age groups, and both sexes. The only class which remains definitely unconvinced and which is un‐ willing to substitute the new noneconomic social superi‐ ority for its economically determined position, is the class of entrepreneurs and industrialists. They sense in the new noneconomic basis an attempt to deprive them of their economic substance, leaving them with an empty though honored title. They are the only group which still believes in the society of Economic Man, since they benefited from it both in economic and social positions. But the other classes, who believe that they can only gain through a divorce of social from economic position, are far more ready to let themselves be persuaded.

Yet at best these attempts are a poor substitute for the real thing. They compensate for economic inequality but do not remove it as a factor of social distinction. They are effective in the same way in which an insurance pay‐ ment may be considered adequate compensation by a man who has lost a leg in an automobile accident; yet no insurance payment will ever give him a new leg. Even the complete success of these attempts would therefore not be enough. They might theoretically give all classes an equality in social fundamentals, sufficient to compen‐ sate them for their inevitable rigid economic inequality.

But they cannot provide a clear-cut, constructive principle of social organization which would give the individual rank and function in a noneconomic society under a noneconomic order of values. Their failure to provide such a new principle is clearly shown in the declining influence of the semimilitary organizations in spite of their steadily increasing numerical strength and their growing emphasis upon the satisfaction of social envy. The place of the "radicals" who built up these organizations and who were mostly killed in the "Roehm purge" of 1934 has been taken by even more revolutionary "radicals." But these new extremists do not content themselves with a noneconomic compensation for economic inequality. Side by side with the continuing unequal, economically determined industrial society, they try to build a completely new society on a noneconomic basis, to which they want to accord supremacy.

The attempts to build a new noneconomic society go back to the war and the immediate postwar years. Then small informal and unorganized groups of men were formed spontaneously on the basis of the common war experience which had transgressed all economic barriers. Even before the war the German Youth Movement had tended to produce similar associations out of the common experience and enthusiasm of youthful romanticism. There the revolt against frozen conventions was used as a noneconomic basis of social organization

which, it was hoped, would permeate, reform, and re-
vitalize all society. The experience which the Nazis had
with the semimilitary organizations which tried to base
themselves unsuccessfully upon the same principle
showed, however, that society cannot be built upon a
purely romantic concept. Though the "Maennerbund"
("the men's association") still plays a large part in
fascist phraseology, it completely failed to be socially
effective. Yet it pointed toward the sphere in which a
realistic noneconomic basis was to be found: the nation
in arms. For a modern army, raised by general conscription, is the only organism in modern society apart
from the churches in which function, rank, and distinction are not by necessity based upon economic position.

Totalitarian *Wehrwirtschaft*—the organization of the
entire economic and social life upon military lines—
serves therefore the vital social purpose of supplying a
noneconomic basis of society while leaving unchanged
the façade of industrial society. At the same time it
serves the no less important purpose of creating full
employment and thereby banishing the demon of unemployment. This does not mean that the Italian and
German armament drives do not serve military ends.
Even if their ultimate purpose is conceived as purely
social, the very pressure of such enormous war machines
would make their eventual use inevitable. But there is
no such thing as a "purely military end" of military

organization. All military organization is not only constructed upon the same principle as the peacetime society which it mirrors, but it also serves the same social ends and ideas. The armies of Napoleon served certainly the most tangible military purposes. Yet their organization did mirror faithfully the new society of the French Revolution in their formal equality—the equal chance for a marshal's baton. They also served a vital social purpose as the one field in which formal equality was real equality. The volunteer armies of Prussia and Austria which rose against Napoleon served as much the social purpose of freeing the Prussian and Austrian middle classes as the military purpose of fighting the French. Similarly, conscription in England during the World War, though enacted for purely military reasons, destroyed or at least seriously weakened the privileged position of the aristocracy. And the drafting of women into war work brought female suffrage. How much more prominent must be the social purpose in a type of military organization which aims at making everybody at all times a soldier!

Moreover, in Germany as well as in Italy military considerations have been subordinated wherever they conflicted with the paramount social purpose of noneco- · nomic organization. The well-known opposition of the army leaders to the fascist and Nazi radicals might be put down as the jealousy of an aristocratic caste against upstarts. But long before the Nazis came to power the German General Staff had decided not to return to a conscripted mass army which they considered a serious military drawback and entirely unsuitable for modern warfare. Their ideal ever since the war has been a small, highly trained and privileged force comprising long-term professional officers and technicians and supplemented by a conscripted militia on the Swiss model which would only be trained for a few weeks or months. In their opinion such a militia would be sufficient to hold the frontiers and to consolidate whatever gains the small, highly mechanized and mobile fighting units would make. And the repetition of the World War mistake, when Germany was defeated by her inability to feed an immobilized war machine, would be avoided. Although the Italian High Command has been unable to express itself in public for a long time, its original concept of "total war" was the same. The experiences in Ethiopia as well as in Spain must have lent strength to the original view. Nevertheless Italy and Germany adopted the mass army.

As far as material rearmament is concerned, it is common knowledge in Germany that the High Command has all along been condemning "military autarchy" as disastrous from a military point of view. The best brains of the General Staff are even said to consider superior the British method of creating potential capacity for wartime production by building "shadow factories" and preserving raw material and currency reserves. The German system, on the other hand, eats up all raw material and foreign exchange reserves in order to produce huge quantities of arms which become rapidly obsolete. This report is borne out by the fact that the German High Command has already twice been changed abruptly when the generals refused to run the risk of war under the *Wehrwirtschaft* organization of the military machine. It is significant that the only branch of the German armed forces which co-operates wholeheartedly with *Wehrwirtschaft* is the air force—the one newly created service which has been staffed almost exclusively from the lower middle classes, who are still largely barred from positions of command in army and navy.

The substance of *Wehrwirtschaft* is the attempt to make all social relationships conform to the model of the relationship between superior and subordinate officer, and between officer and men. It tries to substitute the authority of command for that of economic privilege, the distinction of military rewards for that of economic rewards, the honor code of an army for private profit motives, the function of the individual soldier for that of the worker at the assembly line. Submission under economic dependence, inequality of economic rewards, and discipline of mass-production industry are affirmed as serving not economic but military ends. *Wehrwirt-*

schaft treats the whole country as one army. It cannot tolerate any "civilian"—not even the infant in arms. It must put journalists in uniforms because it cannot recognize a single profession without place and justification in the military organization. It must subject the employer to a military code of honor and make him answerable to martial law. For the sole basis of his authority over the workers must lie in his spiritual and technical "fitness for battle."

At first sight it might appear that, as the Marxists assert, *Wehrwirtschaft* is but a cloak for the complete enslavement of the worker under the capitalist expropriator. It destroys all his liberties and suppresses his trade-unions. The worker is not allowed to strike. He has to work as many hours as he is told to. He may not give notice to his employer or accept work at another plant. He is not allowed to move from one town to the other without a permit; nor may he leave the country. Salaried employees have been treated similarly so that it might seem as if their social and political proletarianization fulfils the forecasts of Marxist theory regarding their ultimate fate under capitalism.

But the new principle of social organization also implies that whatever sacrifices are necessary in the "economic battle" have to be borne above all by the privileged class, in the same way in which officers have to volunteer for very dangerous exploits in warfare in order to keep up the morale of their men. If the "economic battle" threatens heavy losses, the "economic officers" must man the front line in order to stave off a mutiny. We shall see that the economics of *Wehrwirtschaft* apply this principle so that a very real and very sharp impoverishment of the upper and upper-middle classes results therefrom.

The principle of *Wehrwirtschaft* further requires from the employer the same kind of submission under the "commander in chief" to which it subjects the workers. It is a hierarchy in which every member from the lowest to the highest is not allowed any independence or freedom of decision whatsoever. He has to follow blindly the commands of his superior officer. Translated into economic terms, this means that the employer has no longer any freedom or control. He too has to follow orders without answering back even when they disregard his personal and economic interests and insist only on the interests of the whole social army. The industrialist will not be consulted but will receive commands without further explanation. They do not even come from an authority within the economic process but from one without and above it—for instance from the General Staff or from a civil servant. Moreover, the employer is liable to be "transferred" both bodily and economically. In economic terms this means that he will have to dispose of his property whenever the government says so, and that the government decides arbitrarily whether his factory is unnecessary and ought to shut down or whether he is to double his capacity.

Actually, the businessman is as unfree as his workers. He can neither hire nor fire without a government permit. He must not try to entice an employee away from a competitor. He is told what wages to pay. The price at which he sells his products is arbitrarily fixed. In several of the largest industries—for instance, building material, shoes, and fertilizers—the fixed price at which they must execute orders is considerably below cost price. In the case of government orders the industrialist is simply commandeered and told what to produce and at what price. Incidentally, up to 80 per cent of all orders are government orders. In the export business, a board on which the exporter is not represented decides whether he has to accept an order and how much he has to contribute toward the export subsidy for the entire industry. The quality and quantity of his production are fixed by orders from above which he cannot disregard since he receives neither raw materials nor credit in excess of his schedule. His production is not determined by any business considerations, but only by the importance of his product for the whole body economic—tempered sometimes by regard for the maintenance of full employment. Symbolic of the complete subjugation of the employer under noneconomic totalitarianism was the sudden drafting of the best workmen into forced labor on the fortifications in the summer of 1938. During the absence of the workers, their original employers not only had to pay their wages but also had to keep their places open.

In spite of the complete loss of control and freedom of decision on the part of the capitalist, some people still call this system "capitalism" because it retains the principle of private profits. In my opinon the retention of this principle proves absolutely nothing. Under modern economic conditions private profits have ceased to be a constitutive element of society. They are nothing but a lubricant which makes the machine run smoother. Moreover, in a closed economy like the fascist state, which forbids capital exports and enforces compulsory investment, profits are reduced to the status of a bookkeeping entry. Instead of abolishing profits in the first place, the government lets them circulate once more through the economic system, only to regain them in the form of taxes and compulsory loans. In addition, profits are so completely subordinated in Germany and Italy to the requirements of a militarily conceived national interest and of full employment that the maintenance of the profit principle is purely theoretical. Profits have lost their autonomy as an independent, not to say the supreme, goal of economic activity. In most cases they have become a substitute for a management fee—with the one qualification, however, that under fascism the owner-manager bears the full risk. There is a definite trend in Italy and Germany to eliminate profit participation and the ownership rights of nonmanaging partners and shareholders. The manager of a business, regardless of whether he is the owner or only a paid executive, has been freed from all responsibility toward the outside shareholders, even toward a nonmanaging majority owner. If he does not want to pay dividends though the profits would allow it, and prefers to invest in government loans, the government permits him to vote himself a substantial bonus. At the time of writing, a proposal is being discussed in Germany to force the banks to forego their dividend claims "voluntarily" in favor of the government. Since the banks are the largest nonmanaging shareholders in practically all German corporations and are majority owners of more than half, the proposal would effectively abolish the greater part of private corporation profit without touching the abstract principle of private profits at all.

Whatever this system is, it is certainly not capitalist. It is an industrial system of production in which the economic basis has been substantially eliminated. Everyone is subject to the national interest as expressed in terms of military exigency and military organization. Of course, there are profiteers—armament manufacturers, foreign exchange dealers on the "black bourse," or the people who finance the "Aryanization" of Jewish businesses in return for 15 per cent interest and a 25 per cent participation in the profits. But these are phenomena of war economy—regardless of the structure of the economic system that wages war—rather than of capitalism. Anyhow, these profiteers are periodically squeezed out whenever a party official needs money.

The noneconomic structure of *Wehrwirtschaft* becomes even more apparent if we analyze the social status of the other classes: the farmers and the professional middle classes.

The regimentation of agriculture was in both fascist countries the first, and for a considerable time the most drastic, intervention in the free play of economic forces. In either country, and especially in Germany, the threat of the industrial revolution in agriculture had reached a point at which government intervention in the social structure of farming was entirely unavoidable. The introduction of large-scale industrial organization would have converted the majority of German farms into factories producing high-quality foodstuffs for export and domestic consumption on the basis of cheap, imported raw materials. A minority would have been turned into factories for the production of low-grade agricultural raw materials such as rye, potatoes, or sugar beets. In Italy the ratio between "grain factories" and "high-grade factories" would have been the reverse. But in both countries the independent farmer as well as the large feudal landowner would have been destroyed in the name of economic progress. Their place would have been taken by a capital-intensive, industrial undertaking employing largely seasonal proletarian labor.

This sacrifice of their security to the god of progress appeared to the farmers as well as to the big landowners as utterly senseless, since progress had lost its social promise. They therefore unanimously opposed industrialization. Their community of interest explains the united front between small farmers and big landowners who had hitherto always fought each other. However, in spite of their opposition, the revolutionary economic forces gained ground rapidly. In Germany industrial organization on the basis of imported raw material and unskilled labor conquered the hog-raising districts in the Northwest. In the East "grain factories" began to threaten the big estates. In the Southwest fruit-growing was converted into a capitalist and industrialist enterprise. In Italy industrial organization had begun to make inroads in the northern plains; grain factories had been established in the South. The agricultural population saw itself pushed into a war against all the other classes should it want to defend its social status. To force economic progress upon agriculture the government would have had to fight a peasant revolt. To prevent the victory of the industrializing forces the government would have had to give economic support to the existing organization of farming and to endow it with a new social substance. But it could not have remained inactive. And, since none of the other classes believed sufficiently strongly in progress to agree to the first alternative, the regimentation of agriculture became inevitable.

In both countries the regimentation was undertaken under the slogan of "military autarchy." But in both it runs counter to the exigencies of war economy. To ensure maximum production and efficiency in time of war, farming in Germany and Italy would have to be put on a mass production basis strikingly similar to that demanded by economic progress. Capital-intensive production of foodstuffs under a factory system is the only way in which either country can hope to raise enough food in wartime without reducing its supply of man power for the fighting forces. Of course, military efficiency would have demanded a different ratio between high-quality and low-quality products. It would have required more low-quality foodstuffs in Germany, less in Italy; but the principle would have been the same.

The demands of military exigency were satisfied in one respect only: the German farmer has been forced to shift his production from high-quality goods to bulk crops. Otherwise regimentation paid no heed to economic or military requirements. The image of army organization in the regimentation of agriculture was therefore drawn upon only to justify the maintenance of the existing economic and social façade. The peasant fights "a battle"; he is the "first soldier of the Third Reich," or the infantry which mans the front lines of the nation in arms. This pseudo-military function together with the noneconomic task of the peasant class to serve as "biological backbone of the race" explains the maintenance of the family farm as the unit of production. It also justifies the preservation of the large estates—provided they are owner-managed. Hence farms have become inalienable—they cannot be split, sold, or mortgaged. The farmer has to stay on his farm; he is not allowed to leave it, not even to exchange it for another farm. The quasi-military organization which alone can justify the existing agricultural society necessarily demands the complete submission of the farmer and his blind obedience to orders. He must produce what he is told, he is liable to court-martial if he fails to follow instructions, and he must sell his products to the army-state at whatever price the government sees fit to pay. While his social status has been preserved, the farmer has lost all economic independence.

Lastly, the totalitarian state has had to integrate the free professions into its social scheme. From the military point of view this would have been quite superfluous. An army can use the professions as well for its purposes as feudal society, capitalism, or socialism could use them. However, this very quality of the professions as "free" and capable of integration into any social order makes it imperative for totalitarianism to destroy them. They owe their freedom to the fact that they themselves have a noneconomic social substance—thus threatening the necessary monopoly of totalitarianism. To maintain the free professions, to tolerate a noneconomic social substance based upon the concept of freedom, would preserve the one inner enemy which would inevitably destroy the totalitarian social substance. The significant phenomenon of *Wehrwirtschaft* is therefore not that fascism and Nazism convert the free professional into a paid government employee, not even that the professional classes have been reduced in numbers and economic status as sharply as possible. It is the refutation of the claim of the professions to derive their substance from outside the economic and social system. The subordination of the teachings and theories of law, history, medicine, and economics to the principles of totalitarianism, the proclamation of a specific Nazi theory of physics or of mathematics as opposed to the "liberal" theory, the denial of any objective scientific standard or of any absolute knowledge, all express the consequences of the fascist endeavor to exclude all other noneconomic fundamentals of social position. As such the subordination of the professions is the necessary and logical last step toward endowing the noneconomic society of *Wehrwirt-*

schaft with a complete ideological background. Totalitarianism would be contradictory without it; with it the conception of the nation in arms becomes remarkably consistent.

This totalitarian society treats economic objectives as entirely secondary. Before the validity of its social substance can be discussed the question must be answered, what the *economics* of such a society are, especially whether economic goals can be subordinated without courting economic disaster.

Totalitarian economics are generally regarded as a mystery. It is to them that the term "miracle" is usually applied. Actually they are perfectly simple, perfectly rational, and without any trace of the miraculous. They are the one part of the totalitarian system which is ruthlessly logical, as they are entirely based upon the most orthodox economic theories. The fundamental difference between them and the economics of free capitalism is their subordination of all economic aims to the one social end: full employment. Economic progress and increasing wealth are incidental.

The basic innovation of totalitarian economics is, paradoxically enough, a return to the most fundamental tenet of classic economics: that only an increase in investment in capital goods can create employment. This might sound like a truism. But it implies the direct and uncompromising rebuttal of the modern theories according to which economic activity is a function of consumption. Before they came to power the Nazis themselves had officially adopted this modern "underconsumption" theory which holds that depressions stem from a lack of purchasing power. Their whole economic policy has, however, been based upon the opposite view: that depressions are caused by too much consumption and too little investment in producers' goods industries. Hence their conclusion that full employment can be restored only by increasing that quota of the national income which is not consumed but which goes into "savings." This means that the quota available for consumption has to be artificially reduced. The secret of totalitarian economics lies in a "managed consumption." Their success in reducing consumption explains why they could seemingly "create" capital for investment in capital goods industries; whereas, the democracies with all their surplus capital, failed in their attempts to restore full employment by increasing the consumption and the purchasing power of the masses.

Neither in its theoretical approach nor in its methods of consumption-management has totalitarianism been original. Both have been imported almost unchanged from Soviet Russia. Although the underconsumption theory of the business cycle is a Marxist article of faith, Russia had adhered to the opposite theory for more than six years before Hitler came to power. Ever since the

Soviet embarked upon the first Five-Year Plan they have been financing their capital investments by artificial and compulsory reduction of purchasing power and of consumption: through compulsory deliveries of foodstuffs at artificially low prices which do not give the farmers full purchasing power for industrial products; through forced labor; through compulsory loans and compulsory "voluntary" contributions; through the rationing of all articles of consumption, and so on. The Communists had also shown that a managed consumption economy must have a foreign trade monopoly—or at least complete foreign trade control—in order to prevent the diversion of available capital into unwanted consumption. This is important because domestic consumption goods must necessarily become more expensive under a system that devotes all energies to investment in capital goods. The Russians had also proved that such a system needs a stringent foreign exchange control in order to prevent a flight of capital which would foil any attempt to force investment. And, finally, Russia discovered that a policy which regards maximum investment as a supreme goal regardless of private profits must intervene arbitrarily into profits and losses of the individual enterprise and of the individual industry. For the investment which has the greatest effect will invariably be the one which operates at the lowest profit.

Totalitarian economics—first in Germany, later in

Italy—have consciously or subconsciously adopted all these Russian methods and experiences. In their practical application, however, there is one fundamental difference between the communist and the fascist experiment. The Communists had to enforce compulsory savings of capital mainly by reducing the consumption of the peasants and the unskilled workers. In the first place, there were very few others, since Russia was a precapitalist country without a middle class. Secondly, the new ruling and middle classes of the bolshevist army and bureaucracy which emerged after the revolution had to be given economic privileges, compensations, and rewards, since communism is based upon an economic concept of society. The various economic premiums which constitute such a prominent feature of Soviet social life—such as the right to purchase in special stores at special prices— are the means by which the privileged classes are accorded partial or total exemption from the compulsory reduction in the consumption of the whole nation. The fascist countries, on the other hand, had large upper and middle classes whose standard of living was very considerably above the minimum, and whose consumption could be materially decreased before it would approach the level at which there will either be open political opposition or danger of actual starvation. Moreover, fascist society is based upon a noneconomic concept of society—that of the nation in arms. It follows therefrom that the privileged classes are not only the first ones to make sacrifices, but that their very privileges rest upon their readiness to make greater sacrifices than the others. In the communist, economically-conceived society, economic sacrifices degrade socially. In the totalitarian society they raise the social status and strengthen the title to social command and power. We have therefore the paradox that under communism, with its message of economic equality, economic privileges must be given; whereas, under totalitarian fascism, with its preservation of the existing unequal system of industrial production, a disproportionate reduction of the standard of living of the privileged classes tends to establish a distinct trend toward economic equality. However, it must be understood that this trend does not promote social equality. It is precisely because social rank is divorced from economic position that a greater economic equality has become possible.

It must also be understood that this trend toward greater economic equality does not lead to an absolute increase in the economic status of the lower classes. The economic condition of the very lowest classes has probably been improved under fascist rule. The unskilled and semiskilled workers who had been particularly hard hit by unemployment benefited most from the restoration of full employment. The money income of the working class as a whole has risen considerably, and the money income of the individual worker has not been cut in Germany—and comparatively little in Italy. But the workers have been deprived of the increase in income which would have been their due as a result of the increase in industrial activity and output. They have suffered little economic loss, although the "voluntary" contributions to party funds take a goodly slice out of their pay envelopes. But they work longer hours for the same pay. And they would receive at least 20 per cent more if their share in the national income had been maintained at the 1932 level. This alone has probably increased by some 10 per cent the capital available for investment in producers' goods industries.

Several attempts have been made to explain the totalitarian economic "miracle" as due exclusively to this compulsory sacrifice of the working classes. But these attempts do more than violate reality. They are contradictory in themselves and only make fascist economics appear a genuine miracle. How could an increase in investment have been financed by withholding from one class the profits only to be produced through this investment?

The truth is that all the other classes have sacrificed far more than the workers. They have not only been cheated out of profits, but have been forced to cut down on present consumption. The reductions have been the more severe the higher their standard of living used to be, that is, the more privileged they used to be. In the first place, the purchasing power of their incomes has been very sharply cut. Both in Germany and in Italy great care has been taken to keep unimpaired the purchasing power of the mark or lira of the lower classes. The staple foods of the lower classes—bread, potatoes, margarine, cheese, and beer in Germany; cereals, cheese, and wine in Italy—have not been increased in price and are alone available in satisfactory quantities. But meat, butter, fresh fruits, vegetables, eggs, and milk—the high-quality foods of the upper and middle classes—have either disappeared altogether or have become increasingly expensive. The same has happened with almost all articles of consumption. The goods consumed by the lower classes are reasonably plentiful and cheap; the high-quality goods for the higher classes are either nonexistent or very expensive. Hand in hand with this goes rationing. In Germany and Italy most of the higher-grade consumption goods can be bought only at the shop to which the individual has been assigned, and only in limited quantities which are the same for everyone.

In the totalitarian countries no less than in Russia money has therefore a different purchasing power, depending upon the social status of the owner. The one difference is that in Italy and Germany it is the privileged classes whose money has the proportionately lower purchasing power. The actual reduction of their purchasing power has resulted in an "underconsumption" which has released large sums for investment. But even more important as a source of investment capital is the direct reduction of the money income of the upper classes. The typical capitalist income from capital investments has been cut sharply. Dividends are fixed at a maximum of 6 per cent, or, in some cases, of 8 per cent. All surplus profits have to be invested in government loans, which in turn are used for capital goods production. In Italy three capital levies upon corporations have been imposed in succession. In both countries corporation taxes have been raised to almost incredible levels.

In addition to this curtailment of corporate income, the income of the individual member of the upper and middle classes has been pared down—partly by reducing his gross income, partly by increasing taxes and contributions. Hardest hit have been the professional middle classes and the small tradesmen with reductions in net incomes ranging up to 60 per cent. Whereas before Hitler an annual income of 9000 marks was regarded as only fair for the average physician, most German doctors are "expected" at present to contribute all income above 6000 marks to the party. Similar "expectations" apply to lawyers. A German lawyer—moderately well-off and living in a medium-sized town—told me that while his gross income had declined almost 35 per cent since 1933, his taxes and contributions had increased by more than 60 per cent so that they take almost two-fifths of his income. Civil servants' salaries have been cut just as drastically. Most small shopkeepers have been converted into badly-paid government employees whose income has been fixed regardless of their capital investment and former profits. In addition, the burden of "voluntary contributions"—usually prescribed from above—keeps on growing. All professional people and all senior employees in private business or public office are "expected" to hand over at least 15 per cent of their salaries —usually more.

Most, if not all, businessmen and industrialists have been affected in the same way. Gross profits have increased—though not at the rate at which industrial activity has expanded. But the net income of the individual entrepreneur has in most cases become much smaller, as the successful businessman, in addition to being highly taxed, is expected to show his gratitude to the regime in power by sharing with the state and with the party. His contributions—apart from taxes—may approach 40 per cent of his gross income; and it is easier to dodge taxes than to escape the mildly conveyed hint as to the amount one is expected to pay, especially as there is no appeal against this assessment.

All these measures have enabled the totalitarian states to cut consumption by about one-quarter and to double the amount of capital available for investment in capital goods. More than half of the annual national income is thus being "saved." This explains why in an economy which so obviously lives off its capital as does the German, savings and insurance contracts continue to increase.

In addition to consumption-cutting as means to create full employment, totalitarian economics were able to force idle capacity and existing reserves into production. Fascism had to develop some techniques of its own for this purpose; for Russia, starting from scratch, did not have to cope with the problem. First, all private borrowing on the capital market was forbidden, thus conferring upon the government a monopoly for its loans and enabling it to prevent investments in other than *Wehrwirtschaft* capital goods industries. At the same time all savings in banks, savings banks, and insurance companies were forcibly invested in government loans for the financing of armaments. The manufacturers have been forced to hand over their reserves to the government; they have to take long-term government paper in payment against government orders. They are allowed to sell or to discount these bills only if they can prove that they have no reserves. The rapid accumulation of such bills at the banks suggests that by now most manufacturers have already invested all their reserves in these compulsory loans.

Finally, industry has been forced by direct compulsion to finance capital goods investments. The substitute industries, the low-grade iron works, the coal hydrogenation plants, have all been financed through a direct levy. But private industry will not participate in any profits, whereas it will have to bear the full risks. Moreover, the businessman is forced to create employment directly at his own expense through maintaining the army of civil servants, party officials, and private employees engaged in controlling the "planned economy." In Germany about two million people—15 per cent of all people in employment—are needed for this control.

Contrary to general opinion, the expropriation of the Jews and the imminent expropriation of the Catholic Church in Germany do not fall into the same category. Apart from being much below even the most conservative estimates, both Jewish and Catholic properties had been fully invested, so that their expropriation will not furnish any additional capital. The only economic result will be a reduction in income, that is, in the consumption of the former owners. This reduction is considerable, and the impending recruiting of all male Jews into compulsory convict labor will be equivalent to a substantial increase in the available investment capital. But the economic dislocation resulting from these measures has probably already diminished the total available investment capital proportionately more than can be gained by further expropriation and by cheap forced labor. These expropriations do not, therefore, spring from economic reasons but from social and political ones; the economic consequences are quite incidental. We shall see later that, contrary to general opinion, the whole anti-Semitic policy is not based upon economic envy, but—and this applies even more to the anti-Catholic drive—upon entirely noneconomic social and political considerations.

The main goal—full employment—has been reached in both totalitarian countries. That a substantial number of the unemployed have actually only been spirited away from the economic process and put into military and party service does not diminish the success. For those people feel as effectively employed as if they were used productively; and this is the only thing that counts.

In answering the question whether this economic system can last or whether it has to break down, it must first be understood that totalitarian economics are not inherently inflationary. On the contrary, to finance investments by drawing upon idle reserves and by reducing consumption is by necessity deflationary. The growth of government debt represents a mere transfer of assets from private into government ownership, but not an expansion of credit. Not only is no credit being "created," but the total volume of credit in the national economy is probably being reduced. Even the enormous increase of public debt in Nazi Germany has probably been fully

matched by a decrease in private debt. The velocity of
turnover of money and of bank deposits has almost certainly slowed down. Since even a sizable increase in
total debt and a speeding-up of the velocity of money-
turnover would have been justified considering the sharp
increase in production, the deflation has been rather
stringent. It would have gone even further. But political
opposition to the rapid reduction of consumption forced
the German Government into some genuine credit creation in several instances—which are, however, too unimportant to invalidate the theoretical economic concept or to endanger the practical economic policy.

It is obvious that this system is economically vastly
inferior to free capitalism. But it is also generally
argued that it falls short of the Russian model which
supplied the methods of German and Italian economics.
In Russia, too, consumption has been artificially kept
down in order to release capital for investments; but
there the capital has been invested in economically productive industries. Germany and Italy could not have
followed the Russians in this respect, even if they had
wanted to do so. Since the masses had lost their faith
in economic progress, they would not have been willing
to make the necessary sacrifices in consumption for the
sake of economically productive investment. They could
not have been persuaded or forced to forego present
satisfactions in order to obtain greater *economic* satis-

factions in the distant future. The sacrifices had to be imposed for the sake of a noneconomic goal. Fascist society has to be noneconomic, its goal the military autarchy of *Wehrwirtschaft*.

Theoretically, the Russian investments ought to repay the sacrifices with profit. Consumption and purchasing power should begin to benefit long before they approach the danger zone at which the inability to reduce consumption further threatens economic collapse. The Russian failure to organize production and distribution, the disorganization following the suppression of the private-profit motive and the bureaucratization of business, are arguments not against the economic validity of the system, but only against the Russian ability to handle it. Armaments, on the other hand, definitely do not produce any economic values; economically, they are sheer waste. An economy in which full employment is maintained by the maximum production of armaments must necessarily require continuous subsidies out of consumption to keep going. The stage must ultimately be reached at which consumption cannot be reduced any further.

This argument is, however, as fallacious, economically and socially, as it is plausible. In the first place, it is a mere assumption that armaments are economically more wasteful than the economic uses to which the capital expended upon them would have been put otherwise. There is, strictly speaking, but one kind of economically profitable investment: in goods which produce other, more valuable, goods. On the basis of this definition all consumption—except that part that is absolutely necessary to maintain the health and working power of the individual and to make possible the propagation of the human race—is economically not productive but wasteful. If economically unproductive investments like armaments are financed by cutting out economically equally unproductive surplus consumption, the economic position is not changed. If armaments employ more labor than the production of economically unnecessary consumption goods, the production of armaments is even an economic gain. Economically speaking, it is completely irrelevant whether an investment is made to produce radio sets or guns.

This particular fallacy is due to our disapproval of armaments on political grounds; whereas, we approve of civilian consumption and regard a high standard of luxury consumption as morally and socially desirable. But that has nothing to do with economics. As long as armaments are exclusively financed out of savings in not absolutely necessary consumption, a rearmament policy is economically sound. It imperils the regime only if the people either come to regard the sacrificed luxuries as socially or morally more desirable than armaments, or if consumption is reduced to the point beyond which any further decrease would lead to real want.

Economically, the totalitarian system might be even sounder than a system of free capitalism which arms while maintaining full consumption.

But is there not an economic difference between the Russian economy, which concentrates all energies upon investments in genuinely productive capacity, and the German or Italian economy which only converts economically useless consumption into equally useless production? Against this argument it might well be asked whether "economic productivity" has any meaning in a social system which no longer regards an increase in consumption as the goal of the economic order. For economic productivity means only that the investment will ultimately increase the capacity to consume. Since Germany and Italy officially—and Russia unofficially—have given up the economic goal of increased consumption and of an increased standard of living, economic productivity would appear to have ceased to apply to either of them.

But it can also be questioned whether the Russian system is superior if judged on the basis of old-fashioned economics. In other words, it is a mere assumption that just because Russia professes to invest in order to raise her economic productivity, the Russian investments will not require sacrifices beyond the physical possibility of reducing consumption. On the other hand, that the totalitarian countries admittedly use all their investments for rearmament does not mean that all their expenditure is necessarily wasteful. By far the larger share of the German and Italian investments has gone toward building up substitute industries. Now, according to the only conceivable definition, an industry is a substitute industry as long as it is subsidized out of the national income in order to produce goods which could be obtained cheaper or in better quality elsewhere. Every industry that has been started otherwise than by foreign credits has been a substitute industry to some extent in the beginning. By that definition the Russian industrialization has been "substitute" throughout, as Russia could have obtained all her industrial goods far cheaper, far more advantageously, and in far better quality from abroad, had she concentrated on her agricultural and raw material exports. The real test of economic productivity is whether an industry will ever be able to produce cheaper than the sources of supply which it supplants. In this respect, German and Italian substitute industries seem potentially far more productive than the "economically productive" Russian investments. Such *Ersatz* industries as artificial fibers, synthetic rubber, coal hydrogenation, or even the production of sugar from timber, might well become economically productive in the end. After all, rayon, synthetic nitrate, plastics, beet sugar, aluminum, and even hydroelectric power once started out as "substitutes." Russian industry, on the other hand, could only be made productive if an amount at least equal to the capital already pumped into heavy industries should be invested in manufacturing industries. If this process is delayed for years, the original investment in capital goods industries might have become obsolete and a total loss in the meantime. But in the near future the capital for new investments can only be raised—barring foreign loans—by reducing consumption below the irreducible minimum, which is hardly possible.

The main problem of a "managed consumption" economy lies not in the economic but in the social and political field. As long as the masses are willing to accept a reduction of consumption and as long as they accept as socially more desirable the goods which are produced in the place of former nonessential consumption goods, the system can work. "Guns instead of butter" is not an economic alternative; it is a moral and social choice. Contrary to general opinion, the reduction of consumption is not a weakness of the totalitarian society but one of its main sources of strength. It is the means by which the noneconomic society is balanced. The fact that the standard of living and of consumption of each class is reduced proportionately less than that of the class immediately above, lends economic substance to the substitution of noneconomic for economic rewards. This negative economic compensation is the greatest and the most potent social satisfaction in the noneconomic society of totalitarianism. And it will continue to satisfy the masses until and unless they cease to believe in the ideology of the noneconomic society altogether. The collapse, if it comes, will be a moral and not an economic collapse.

One exception, however, must be stated: the system will break down economically if the irreducible minimum of consumption is reached before an equilibrium between consumption and investment is found which gives full employment without requiring increasing investments. It lies in the nature of totalitarian economics that such an equilibrium cannot be found. Eventually, the economic limit of the managed consumption economy will be reached. But the time which it will take to reach this stage is generally vastly underestimated. Under peacetime conditions the reduction of consumption should not accelerate but decelerate. The momentum of the vicious spiral of impoverishment will never quite disappear; but it should slow down to the extent to which employment is being found. Furthermore, the limit to which consumption can be reduced is usually underestimated by capitalist and socialist observers, who are inclined to regard a high standard of living as a moral good in itself. If, as appears likely, the over-all standard in Germany has declined by some 20 per cent since 1932, a further deterioration of 25 per cent could be enforced by reducing the standard of the upper and middle classes to that of the employed skilled workers. German authorities figure that the total consumption would have to decline by 60 per cent as against 1932 before the whole nation has been reduced to the standard of the lowest group of unskilled workers or of farm hands, assuming that these standards represent the irreducible minimum. In Italy, the margin between present consumption and subsistence level is much narrower. But Italy, being far less industrialized, has to provide far less employment and can, consequently, get along with far less annual reduction of consumption. While, therefore, economic collapse through economic attrition is the ultimate outcome of the totalitarian economic system, it is as little a practical and imminent danger to its continued existence as death from old age is for a boy of eighteen. Too many other and earlier possibilities of political or social collapse threaten, to allow the remote economic peril to become practical politics.

It is, therefore, of the greatest importance that there exists one problem, both in Italy and in Germany, which threatens to accelerate the trend toward ever-increasing reduction of consumption and to decrease consumption quickly to the subsistence level: *the problem of imported raw materials*. To be sure, this problem is not one of the theory of totalitarian economics. In a self-sufficient country it would be nonexistent. For Italy and Germany, with their peculiar geographical and geophysical position, it constitutes the greatest, if not the only, economic problem.

At first glance it is not easy to see why this should be so. On the basis of traditional economics, the internal system of production should not make much difference to the balance of trade. But, while this is correct under the Economics of Increasing Wealth of capitalism and socialism, it is not true under the Economics of Impoverishment of totalitarian fascism. Imports are the only investment which such an economy can finance neither through a reduction of consumption nor through requisitioning idle reserves. Imports have to be paid for in exported goods. These export goods have to come out of that part of the national income that is not invested in capital goods production. To the extent to which this part becomes smaller through the artificial raising of the investment quota in a managed consumption economy, the production of the export goods required to balance imports will take up an increasing share of the freely available, noninvested national income. Unchanged imports will, therefore, represent a growing burden on the economy. An increasing number of domestic goods will have to be produced and an increasing quantity of domestic labor will have to be employed to provide the countervalue for an unchanged quantity of imports. To the extent to which this increase further reduces consumption, it raises in turn the import burden in a vicious spiral that feeds on itself.

In other words, the impoverishment through consumption reduction finds its expression in a tendency toward an unfavorable balance of trade and of prices, which in turn increases the impoverishment, and so on. An exact parallel to this development is furnished by the situation of an agricultural debtor country during a period of falling commodity prices. In order to obtain an unchanged amount of foreign exchange for the service of its debt, such a country has to export an increased quantity of its agricultural products. This creates oversupply and results in a further reduction of the prices for its commodities. The lowered income from its products again increases the quantity which must be exported to realize the original, unchanged amount of foreign exchange, and so on. However, an agricultural debtor country can escape the "debt screw" by default on its debts, without impairing the income of anybody except its foreign creditors. It can shift the reduction in consumption from its own shoulders to that of the outside world. But, if the import-dependent totalitarian country tries to escape from the vicious spiral by reducing imports, the very real danger arises that this will only lead to a further internal decrease in the capital available for consumption and, therefore, to a further internal increase in the costs of production of export goods. Ultimately, this might not only nullify the beneficial effects of the import reduction, but might even lead to a net loss on international balance. Not even the attempt to replace imports by substitute products from new domestic industries need be beneficial. The building of substitute industries itself obviously requires capital investments, which must come out of the free national income, so that the international bargaining position of the country is impaired during this initial period. But after they have begun to produce, substitute industries will be economically beneficial only if they cease to be "substitute" and yield more to the national economy than they require in the form of subsidies, new investments, and depreciation. They might well be beneficial even if the loss arising from the higher costs and the inferior quality of their products outweighs the savings in imports in terms of money. For the burden of the imports which they replace might be—and in most cases actually will be—far heavier than the money-figure expresses. If, however, substitute industries fail to reach the stage at which they cease to be "substitute" in terms of the national economy as a whole, the burden of their maintenance will in time exceed the benefits derived from the replacement of imports, and they will turn into a permanent net loss. This might happen even when substitute industries appear to be actually beneficial for a time after they get into production. Suddenly a critical point will be reached at which their capital requirements begin to increase again, though they should actually decrease. This might be only a temporary disturbance, eliminated after a few years. But it might also be permanent, in which case the import problem becomes economically insoluble. Even if the failure of substitute industries to become economically beneficial is only temporary, the disturbance created thereby is a very serious matter.

This holds true of any managed consumption economy in a country that does not start practically self-sufficient, as Russia did. It applies doubly to a country that concentrates on armaments as capital goods investments, and trebly to Germany and Italy. Armaments have almost the highest ratio between raw material and labor requirements. Moreover, Germany and Italy are completely deficient in the raw materials needed for armaments. Had they concentrated upon skyscrapers as capital goods to provide full employment, they would have needed few imported raw materials; they would then have been able to cut imports and to use all remaining imported goods for consumption. But, concentrating on armaments, they could not cut out raw material imports, and they had, moreover, to divert the use of their imports from consumption into capital goods production. The increase in the burden of imports was doubly accelerated: first by the necessity to maintain the absolute volume in spite of a cumulative increase in the relative burden and secondly by the additional pressure upon consumption resulting from the rerouting of imports into capital goods production.

In Italy the effects of these developments have been concealed by the even greater economic damage caused by the actual state of war in which business has been functioning since the beginning of the Ethiopian campaign. But in Germany it can be clearly seen that the import situation gave increasing momentum to the reduction of consumption and to the deterioration of the country's international economic balance and international purchasing power.

German over-all imports have declined comparatively little since 1933; but, whereas before Hitler about two thirds of the imports were used for consumption and the remainder for the manufacture of more valuable goods for export, more than two-thirds of the present imports are used for military and industrial armament. The result has been a steady increase in the burden of producing the export goods against which imports are obtained. In 1932 it did not take more than one-quarter of Germany's productive capacity to manufacture the necessary exports. According to the best estimates, imports then furnished more than 25 per cent of internal consumption, and Germany's international balance was more or less even—a decline against predepression times, when there had been a heavy surplus, but still quite satisfactory.

At present, imports average less than one-fifth of Germany's annual national income—in consequence of the increase in the nominal national income and the simultaneous, though slight, decrease in imports. But this fifth corresponds to almost half of Germany's "free" production, that is, to that part of production which is not taken up by capital investments. The burden on the actually available national income has thus been practically doubled. Germany must hand over twice as large a part of her production of free goods in order to finance imports which are not consumed.

This situation finds its expression in the steady deterioration of Germany's balance of trade. An even better indication is the steady increase in the subsidy paid to exporters, which now amounts to about 35 per cent of the value of all exports; such a subsidy is obviously a toll on domestic consumption for the financing of raw material imports. It tends, therefore, to decrease consumption further and in turn to make more difficult the problem of paying for imports. Transactions like the purchase of coffee in Brazil against domestically produced German goods have the same vicious effect. The coffee is subsequently dumped on the world market at a very low price in order to obtain foreign exchange wherewith to buy armament materials which cannot be obtained against German products. The loss which the domestic consumer has to carry is all the greater because Germany has to pay more for the coffee than the world market price. She has to hand over her own goods in exchange at prices which lie below those of her foreign competitors.

This situation is even worse than this example indicates. In the first place, Germany can resort to methods of trickery which, though they are necessarily short-lived, alleviate the problem as long as they work. She can use political threats to force the Balkan countries to hand over their raw materials against German goods for which they cannot find any use but which Germany can produce easily. She forces Yugoslavia to accept a quantity of aspirin sufficient to fill her requirements for fifteen years, as "payment" for her copper and wheat. Greece has to take tons upon tons of mouth organs for her tobacco and her raisins. Bulgaria must be satisfied with one million artificial-leather cameras without lenses and without photographic paper, as fair value for her tobacco and meat. These tricks alleviate the import burden very effectively, though only temporarily. They shift the burden of the cut in consumption from the shoulders of the German people to those of the Yugoslav, Greek, and Bulgarian masses. Secondly, Germany has been passing through the stage at which substitute industries seem to become economically profitable as they replace a greater import burden than they cost to build up and to operate. From 1935 to the end of 1937, the rate of increase of the relative import burden tended to slow down. German economists hoped that it would stabilize during 1938. From then onward the absolute import burden was expected to decrease with the anticipated steady reduction of absolute imports. This expectation has proved wrong. At the critical point substitute industries failed. The investment required to keep them going did not fall below their yield in the form of consumption goods. Consequently, the relative import burden has been again sharply increasing. This might be only a temporary trend caused by bad timing of a new substitute industries program; or it might be a lasting trend signifying the inability of Germany to make her substitute industries profitable in terms of national economy. Anyway, the unfavorable trend will continue for some considerable time to come, at least until the new projects themselves reach the critical stage.

As a result of this development of the import problem, the vicious spiral of expropriation and reduction of consumption has been accelerated. In several spheres the irreducible minimum has already been reached. The export subsidy alone has probably expropriated more industrial capital than all requisitioning of idle reserves for capital goods production.

But the most dangerous deterioration has occurred in

agriculture. The failure of the Nazi agricultural policy does not lie in its inability to produce enough domestic high-quality foods like eggs, butter, meat, and fresh fruit to take the place of the former imports. This was expected by the Nazi leaders. They believed, however, that an increase in the domestic production of low-quality bulk foods like grain, potatoes, sugar-beet, and turnips would compensate for these high-grade foods. They achieved a fair measure of success on paper, although the results did not come up to full expectations because of the subordination of economic ends under the social ideology of the family farm. Yet actually there are not more but less bulk foodstuffs available for public consumption, since an increasing share has to be diverted to uses other than consumption, such as storage against future wars, conversion into industrial alcohol to replace imported gasoline, or the production of plastics and synthetic lubricants. Consumption has therefore not only been reduced by the amount of high-quality foodstuffs formerly imported, but also by a not inconsiderable amount of low-quality foodstuffs, although their total production has been increased.

Whereas the supply of food for human consumption is still capable of further reduction before the subsistence minimum is reached, the supply of fodder is critically near its lowest limit. Before 1933 about 35 per cent of all fodder had to be imported. These imports have been almost completely eliminated, and the foreign exchange has been diverted to imports of armament material. In addition, the supply of domestic fodder for consumption of privately owned cattle has been continuously declining in spite of an increase in total production by 20 to 30 per cent. The German fodder supply has almost reached the point beyond which cattle would actually starve. The situation is as bad as it was in 1917, and it is steadily deteriorating.

But the percentage of agricultural products that has to be imported has not declined and still averages about 30 per cent of the total consumption of foodstuffs. Of course, these 30 per cent represent a much smaller absolute quantity as total consumption has gone down. But the economic effort necessary to pay for the so much reduced quantity is probably not smaller than in 1932, but greater. In spite of all sacrifices, the dependence on imports has, therefore, not become smaller, but probably even larger. Longer hours have to be worked and more export goods have to be produced in order to provide the foreign exchange for the present foodstuff imports.

Even more important than the direct economic threat are the political and social consequences and repercussions of the import problem. As far as military strength goes, the import question has probably not only nullified the increase in strength resulting from armament, but has resulted in an absolute weakening of the war strength; for an increased import burden is a very serious military handicap in warfare.

In addition, the implications of the import situation greatly influence foreign policy up to the point where they enforce a complete revision of foreign aims. If substitute industries fail to solve the import problem, it can only be overcome by shifting the burden of consumption from the shoulders of the domestic masses to those of the raw material producers. As long as the relationship between the consumer and the producer of raw materials remains entirely commercial, this cannot be done for any length of time, whatever degree of economic imperialism and economic penetration prevails. Dr. Schacht's methods of trade, which have made all raw-material producing countries eager to sell to other markets if they can be found, would collapse as soon as world trade recovers. Totalitarian trade policy, therefore, must aim at the political subjugation of the raw material producers, which will make them a part of the domestic economy. And even that would not be enough; for the raw material producers are likely to refuse cuts in their consumption unless they are convinced of the desirability of their ultimate purpose. They must therefore be forced to accept themselves the totalitarian ideology of the noneconomic society.

The characteristic of totalitarian foreign politics does

not lie in its methods. After all, these are the same as those used by every aggressive Power in the absence of determined resistance, from the days of the Romans down to the French procedure over the Ruhr in the postwar years. What constitutes a real innovation is the ideological imperialism of totalitarian foreign policy. For economic reasons alone fascist and Nazi foreign policy must tend to work by revolutionary means in order to conquer a country from within. It used to be said of British imperialism in the past that "it says Christianity and means cotton"; the present-day trade policy of the totalitarians says "cotton" but means "fascist revolution in order to get the cotton."

This connection between the economic situation and the foreign policy explains why Germany had to revive the demand for colonies and why she cannot be satisfied with any international administration of colonial raw material resources. Yet the demand for colonies is highly unpopular within Germany, because the German people feel very little attracted by the tropics. Also, it runs counter to Hitler's most cherished and most sensible foreign political goal: the lasting alliance between a British Empire that rules the seas and a German Empire that rules the Continent.

In Europe too, particularly in the Balkans, Germany cannot be satisfied with concessions or even with political, military, and commercial predominance. She must enjoy full political control to the extent that she can induce the Balkan masses to shoulder a part of the reduction of consumption which is necessary for the maintenance of the German economic system. That means, in the first place, that the Balkan masses must be converted to the totalitarian ideology and, secondly, that the Balkan upper and middle classes must be expropriated, since the standard of living of the lower classes on the Danube cannot be reduced any further. Germany therefore tries to conquer the Balkans by capturing the latent forces of peasant revolution against the land-owning and industrial classes.

Finally, the import problem imperils the noneconomic totalitarian society itself at its weakest spot: farming. It tends to introduce the very "industrial" methods of agricultural production which to prevent was one of the main tasks of fascism. Under the pressure of agricultural demand, methods have been inaugurated in parts of southwest Germany which are identical with those of the Soviet collective farm in everything but name. They retain private ownership of farm land as a mere title; but they provide for mechanized, impersonal, and labor-saving methods of work on what is to all intents and purposes a government-owned agricultural factory which employs the former farmers as landless laborers. In East Prussia the traditional province of big feudal estates, "grain factories" are cropping up. Under the title of "farm set-

tlement" large estates are taken over by the government
—with or without compensation—and discharged professional soldiers are settled on them. Legally these new
settlers hold the land as independent individual owners
or as hereditary tenants. Actually, they are workers
under the command of a government manager. Not without reason has Dr. Darré, the Nazi Minister of Agriculture, warned for years against the impending bol-
shevization of German agriculture.

However, in spite of its implications, the import problem is not a vital problem of totalitarian society as such.
It is solvable precisely because it is not a problem that
is inherent in totalitarian economics. It is inherent in
the German and Italian situation, but it can be overcome
by changes in the external relations of these two countries. The economic problems, moreover, only accelerate
and strengthen the dynamic social and political forces
inherent anyhow in totalitarianism.

Neither the validity of the totalitarian miracle nor the
stability of the totalitarian society are, therefore, proved
or disproved by economics. These decisive questions depend entirely upon whether totalitarianism can perform
its social and political miracle, whether it can banish
the demons and restore the rationality of society and of
the world.

CHAPTER SEVEN

MIRACLE OR MIRAGE?

THE noneconomic society of *Wehrwirtschaft* succeeds in exorcising the demon of unemployment. But in itself it can be successful and can prove its validity only if war—the other demonic threat to modern society—can be made to appear not only rational and sensible but definitely desirable. If war is accepted as an end in itself —in the same way in which bourgeois democracy and Marxist socialism accept economic progress as an end in itself—the fascist task is accomplished. Class war and economic inequality would have ceased to be of importance in the noneconomic society. Otherwise the totalitarian miracle must fail.

The consistent new concept of society which totalitarianism proclaims is nothing but a mirage unless war is accepted not only as legitimate but as supreme. Man's function and his place in war must lay the basis of his function and place in society altogether. Hitler's and Mussolini's entire social and political edifices are necessarily built upon Heroic Man as the concept of man's true nature.

Mussolini's "live dangerously" and Hitler's constant railing against the "bourgeois with his umbrella" are therefore meant as fundamental expressions of a new creed. The anonymous soldier in the trenches, the equally anonymous worker on the assembly line, are fundamental symbols of this new concept of man. And Ernst Juenger, the one really profound German philosopher of the totalitarian state, has therefore consciously based his new society upon the figure of the Worker-Soldier; physical pain and the ability to endure it are the basis of his new order of values.

The central theory of the fascist concept of Heroic Man is the self-justification of personal sacrifice—one of the oldest and most deeply-rooted ritual concepts of mankind, which has always been used to placate or to banish demonic forces. This conception captured a large part of the postwar youth, both in Italy and Germany. After the World War had revealed its irrationality and folly, it became unendurable to declare as utterly senseless and in vain the terrible slaughter and the annihilation of the best sons of the nation. Their sacrifice came to be held its own justification. The symbol of this spirit was the glorification of Langemarck, a battle in the first weeks of the war in which thousands of young German students, fresh from the recruiting depots, were sent, virtually unarmed, into certain death from enemy artillery and machine guns. That there was no military purpose whatever to this hecatomb which was owing to the mistake of some commanding officer, only heightened its symbolic character as "pure sacrifice."

Only through the sublimation of a senseless immola-tion into a magical offering can the very elements of irrational warfare be rationalized again. The isolation of the individual in machine war, the anonymity of his sacrifice, and the blind arbitrary rule of fate appear as ends in themselves in the self-justification of individual sacrifice.

It is a common and stupid mistake to look at this exaltation of sacrifice in totalitarianism as mere hypoc-risy, self-deception, or a propaganda stunt. It grew out of deepest despair. Just as nihilism in the Russia of 1880 attracted the noblest and bravest of the young people, so in Germany and Italy it was the best, not the worst, representatives of the postwar generation who re-fused to compromise with a world that had no genuine values worth dying for and no valid creed worth living for. And like the Nihilists the Fascists believe with re-ligious fervor, genuine conviction, and complete un-selfishness in the self-justification of sacrifice. In the whole Nazi movement there are probably no men more sincere than those few Elite Guardists who have fore-sworn the will to live and have mastered death by their readiness to sacrifice themselves. All the others are just camp followers, "Sunday Nazis," as they are contemptuously called by the radicals who believe fervently in the sacrifice.

From a moral point of view the concept of Heroic Man might therefore appear valid, as it might give purport and sense to the individual. But it cannot give purport and sense to society. Because it denies life, the self-justification of sacrifice not only denies but destroys society. To live dangerously may be all right for the individual; but a society has, above all, to live continuously, and that means safely. If the individual finds his satisfaction and his fulfillment in suicide, then society can have no meaning at all. And anarchy must appear to be the only legitimate form of social existence.

It is this inner conflict that has foiled the fascist attempt to create a new order. Totalitarianism can banish the demon of unemployment and it can restore the rationality of war for the individual. But it cannot effect this rationalization without making society appear irrational and senseless. It cannot perform its miracle.

The inability of fascist ideology to extend the restoration of the rationality of war into the social sphere attests this failure. Some theorists profess to regard war as a constitutive and essential element of society because it destroys society; for societies have to die. But this newest formulation of the cyclical theory of history fails to explain why societies have to live at all. And, though it permeates the whole of contemporary fascist popular

philosophy, the theory has not acquired any strength outside of esoteric and pseudo-scientific periodicals. The
masses have not even been touched by it.

Fascism has therefore been forced to continue the attempt at banishing and outlawing war which had been
made by the preceding regime, although the form differs
considerably from the collective security aims of postwar democracy. Postwar Europe sought to justify its
social order by claiming that it guarantees the real peace.
So fascism tries to justify itself by asserting that only a
fascist country can be peaceful. The "peace-loving leadership" of Germany or Italy is constantly being con-
trasted with the "war mongers" in the democracies. The
freedom from the emotions of the masses which totalitarianism allegedly enjoys is held up against the "mob
rule" of parliamentary majority governments and against
the "unbridled war propaganda" of a free press. If
there could have been any doubt as to whether the fascist
governments owe their popularity to the glorification
of war in the creed of Heroic Man or to the promise to
banish war, the spontaneous and general rejoicing of the
German and Italian people, especially of the youngest
generation, after the Munich accord, and their near-
rebellion in the days before, would have dispelled it. In
spite of all propaganda, the masses in the totalitarian
countries fear war even more than those in the democracies.

This sharp cleavage over the issue of war is not simply a dialectic exaggeration of the old position which regarded war as an evil, though as a smaller evil under certain conditions, and therefore as the *ultima ratio regum*. *Wehrwirtschaft* can be justified only if war is regarded not as evil but as unequivocally good. But the condemnation of war to which the fascist regimes owe their popularity allows of no compromise with the view that war is always an unmitigated evil.

This inevitable failure to base a society on the anarchic concept of Heroic Man vitiates irreparably the entire performance of totalitarian fascism. It renders impossible the successful solution of class war, as it frustrates its replacement by the new social noneconomic harmony of the nation in arms. Arming as a means of exorcising the demons of unemployment becomes as irrational as unemployment itself. This destroys the basis on which alone the sacrifices in consumption are justifiable. Yet armaments must continue as the supreme aim, and the noneconomic society must continue to be based on the nation in arms. For there is no alternative.

In such a situation there is but one way out: to throw the blame on others. The conflicting forces within its society which fascism cannot overcome, resolve or integrate must be converted into enemies threatening from without. War as an intangible demonic force has to be replaced by war as a conspiracy of very tangible persons or groups. Though they arm chiefly for internal social reasons, the totalitarian countries continuously have to invent enemies against whose aggressive designs they have to be prepared. For its own justification fascism must maintain that the others want to attack and that self-defense compels it to arm to the teeth. Fascism must always appear eager to disarm; but it must always appear unable to do so by reason of some pretended danger. It is Abyssinia that intends to attack Italian colonies, Austria that schemes to annex Bavaria by force, Czechoslovakia which provides air fields for the Soviets from which to bomb German towns. Since they cannot build up a positive creed which either glorifies or renounces war, the fascist regimes must resort to a purely negative "holy war" which blames outside elements for the failure to rationalize the demonic forces within fascism.

The clearest expression of this necessity in the field of foreign affairs was the campaign which the Italian government conducted against Anthony Eden as the personal symbol of all the evil forces in the world. He was made responsible for every adverse development—even for the fall in the prices of Italian export products. Similarly, Hitler began to justify German armaments and Germany's war-preparedness with the "conspiracy" of Winston Churchill and Anthony Eden as soon as the German people had shown their decisive rejection of war.

To the extent to which it becomes apparent that totalitarian fascism fails to create a new order, this self-assertion and self-justification in the persecution of personified demons becomes its main, if not its only, creed. The fight against these enemies becomes its only aim. Of course, all revolutions suffer from a persecution complex, sometimes with some reason, sometimes entirely imaginary. But only fascism must see in the persecution of its enemies the substance of its creed. Only in fascism are real persons made to appear solely responsible for the threat to life, security, and sanity of the individual. Their extermination becomes the justification of fascist society. Perpetual unrelenting warfare against them becomes a holy task which not only permits but demands brutality, violence, and deception. In the cosmos of fascism these are not ordinary enemies, but personified demons with whom there can be no truce and no peace. As tangible, rationally comprehensible, and therefore bearable, enemies they are substituted for the intangible, incomprehensible, and therefore unbearable, demonic forces of modern society, for impersonal economic laws or for the unavoidable consequences of industrial imperialism.

The hatred of the Communists signifies the failure to overcome class war in fascist society. As the masses fail to accept the ideology of the nation in arms, class war cannot be abolished. It can only be outlawed as the hostile force to the noneconomic and truly classless society of fascist dreams and promises. It can only be fought by personifying it in the person of the Communists, who have to be made answerable for those sinister forces within fascist society. Fascism requires no proof of any communist action. It is quite irrelevant whether there was really any communist danger during the last years of the German Republic or in postwar Italy. When the Communists were acquitted of having set fire to the German Reichstag, Goering admitted perfectly frankly that in spite of all proof to the contrary Germany would persist in holding them responsible for the arson. For, he added, "We know that the enemy must have come from outside the German people." For its own existence and for its *raison d'être* fascism must have permanently communist conspiracies and alliances between Moscow and all other opponents of fascism— the British bankers or the Czech army, the Catholic Church or the psychoanalysts.

Nazi racial anti-Semitism is the most complete, most consistent, and most perfected form of this personification of the demons which, by rejecting reason, tries to restore the rationality of the world and to justify the Nazi society. Nazi anti-Semitism merits, therefore, extensive analysis not only because of its brutality and cruelty and because it has become the outstanding characteristic of Nazism, but because it expresses better and more pronouncedly than any other feature the inner dynamics and the inner logic of the totalitarian revolution. At the same time it is the least understood angle.

The real function of the Jews and "Non-Aryans" in Nazi theology is the personification of the forces of bourgeois capitalism. Their persecution as "demons" became necessary because Nazism fails to replace the profit motive by some noneconomic motive as the driving force in social relations. Official Nazi theory does not admit this; probably it does not understand it. Its racial theory of the irreconcilable conflict between the Nordic and the Semitic is an appeal to the belief in the miracle. How else can it reconcile the contradiction between the alleged biological superiority of Nordic man and the simultaneous biological superiority of Jewish blood which makes one Jewish grandparent taint irreparably the blood of three Nordic ones? This theory gives, however, no answer to the politically important question why this allegedly fundamental conflict has been released just now and just in this form.

The explanations sought by a puzzled and outraged outside world are equally unsatisfactory. To say that the persecution of the Jews is an outbreak of unprecedented and cowardly brutality is a statement of fact and a just condemnation; but it is no explanation. The view that "Germany was always anti-Semitic" springs from a complete misunderstanding of the prewar and pre-Hitler situation. Of course, there was discrimination against the Jews in prewar Germany and Austria. Of the two attributes of full equality: *connubium* and *commercium*, they did not enjoy full *commercium*. A Jew could not become an officer in the army, a judge, or a university professor. Yet this was a discrimination of creed, not of race. All careers were open practically without restriction to converts who embraced the Christian faith, as very many did. On the other hand, there was full *connubium*, which did not exist elsewhere. Mixed marriages were as common in German-speaking central Europe as they were rare everywhere else. The fact that today the number of Christian Non-Aryans of mixed Gentile-Jewish parentage far exceeds the number of hundred-per-cent Jews, is sufficient proof of widespread intermarriage. As *connubium* is more important socially than *commercium*, the German Jews were justified in their general belief that Germany was the least anti-Semitic country.

Equally misleading is the attempt to explain German anti-Semitism as based upon economic envy, upon the desire to eliminate Jewish competition and to obtain the positions held by the Jews in business and in the professions. It would be foolish to deny that such envy existed. But in only one class did it assume more than minor proportions: the small shopkeepers wanted to rid themselves of the competition of the Jewish-owned department stores. How little this feeling was shared by the great majority of the people became manifest in the overwhelming opposition against Nazi attempts to close down the department stores. Now that they have been "Aryanized" they attract almost as large a share of retail trade as before 1933. On the whole, economic envy was confined to isolated cases, even in the professions where the Jewish share was largest. To complain about Jewish competition in a doctor's or lawyer's club would have been the height of bad taste.

But even if economic envy had been a major cause of the outbreak of anti-Semitism in Germany, it cannot be the cause of its continuation now that the Jews have been deprived of all their property and positions. Most of the people who expected to benefit from the elimination of the Jews must have been bitterly disappointed. Neither did the department stores close down, as the independent retailers expected, nor did the closing of the Jewish-owned retail stores result in an increase in the business of their Gentile competitors. The business of the Jews just disappeared with them. I refuse to believe that any small retailer understands the social and economic conditions of Nazi Germany well enough to realize that the effects of the total shrinkage of retail business on his own business may have been mitigated somewhat by the closing of the Jewish-owned stores. And should he understand so much, he would most certainly draw the conclusion that Nazism, not the Jews, threatens his business—a conclusion which he has not drawn. The same situation exists with regard to the executive positions, the free professions, and the banks. The Jewish-owned private banks have been liquidated, but their business disappeared too. Jewish doctors and lawyers have been excluded, but the business of the Gentile doctors and lawyers, instead of increasing, has decreased. Jewish bank directors have been dismissed, but their jobs have not been filled.

The only anti-Semitic action which benefited more than a handful of people is the very one which not even the most extreme Nazi could have foreseen or believed possible in 1933: the "Aryanization" of small and medium-sized Jewish businesses. Even this measure is a doubtful blessing. For every Gentile manager who could buy the business of his Jewish boss for a song, two Gentile managers have lost their jobs through "Aryanization."

Anti-Semitism, furthermore, is not due to any inherent opposition of the German Jews to the principles of Nazism—except, of course, its anti-Semitism. Had the German Jews been allowed to enlist in Hitler's movement, they would have joined, just as Italian Jews subscribed to Italian fascism as long as they were welcome. The quota of Jews in Nazism probably would have been even higher. For the German Jews were longing for an opportunity to achieve a complete merger with the rest of the German people in a national movement that transcended religious barriers. Not without reason orthodox rabbis, during the first years of the Nazi regime, tended to regard Hitler's anti-Semitism not only as a punishment of the Lord but as His way to save His people from complete loss of identity and of religion.

Lastly, there is the explanation that the Jews are used as scapegoats—a statement which is as correct as it is meaningless. For why does Nazism need a scapegoat, and why the Jews? In 1932 it should have seemed far more sensible to play upon the violent popular indignation against the corrupt municipal governments of the postwar period than to arouse an anti-Jewish sentiment.

The real explanation for racial anti-Semitism in Germany, and even more in Austria, is that the substitution of the Jews for the hostile forces of bourgeois capitalism and liberalism was made possible, if not mandatory, by the unique social structure of the German bourgeoisie. I have explained before that the German bourgeoisie did not attain power by its own revolutionary efforts. Unlike the middle classes in western Europe, it was liberated from above. Its emancipation was not a social end in itself; it was effected for the purpose of national unification. Politically and socially the bourgeoisie therefore never became a ruling class. The aristocracy and the hereditary, though often untitled, nobility of civil servants and officers remained the social and political master.

Accordingly, the typical bourgeois professions did not receive full social recognition. Outside of a few small areas like Hamburg and Frankfurt, with their old trading tradition, the businessman was not accepted as a social equal. Even the banker was only just tolerated in "society." The free professions which in western Europe attained the highest social valuation as the embodiment of all bourgeois ideals, were held in much lower esteem than the badly paid but traditionally valued positions in the army and the civil service. Whereas in France the least-qualified law student went into government service as a police-court judge, the elite of the German students preferred judicial and administrative appointments to the lawyer's profession. In addition, the upper classes actively discouraged the formation of a strong and independent bourgeoisie as potentially dangerous to their rule. Thus the indigenous German bourgeoisie were not only numerically weak and politically impotent but in latent opposition and socially discriminated against. Yet the rapid development of capitalist society required a strong middle class.

The special position of the Jews in Germany stems from this. The German Jews were liberated from above at the same time and by the same forces which liberated the German bourgeoisie. In the western European coun-

tries they were emancipated only long after an indigenous middle class had grown up and had seized
power; there the Jews had to find their place in an already firmly entrenched bourgeois society which regarded them as newcomers and upstarts. In Germany,
however, they and the Gentile bourgeoisie started out
together at the same time. The Gentiles and the Jews met
with the same kind of social and political discrimination
on the part of the ruling classes; and they were forced
into the same opposition. The discrepancy between the
numerical and qualitative demands for a bourgeoisie
and the available supply under the social discrimination
and under the antibourgeois government policy produced an enormous demand for Jewish businessmen,
bankers, lawyers, doctors, and engineers. In Austria,
Bavaria, and Prussia the government even supported
this trend as it was held that a Jewish bourgeoisie would
never, like a Gentile one, incite the people to "dangerous thoughts." Moreover, contrary to the situation in
western Europe, the Jews had been settled in Germany
as long, if not longer than the rest of the population. The
Jewish settlements on the Rhine date back to Roman
times. They spoke the same German language, and everything in their tradition that was not ritual was of German origin.

The result was that German Jews and German Gentiles
merged completely in the socially and politically under-

privileged, but economically and intellectually decisive, upper middle class. The Gentiles regarded the Jews as equal because they suffered the same discrimination and because they opposed it by appealing to the same principles of democracy. On the part of the Jews the equality accorded within the bourgeoisie put an end to that exclusiveness by means of which they have always maintained their inner unity against persecution and discrimination. On both sides business partnerships, closest social intercourse, and mixed marriages came to be regarded as matters of course. The Jews progressively lost their objection against a change of their religion which remained as the only obstacle in the way of full equality within their class. As a result of this development Jewry itself declined; in another fifty or hundred years there would have been hardly any Jews left in Germany or Austria. But in the bourgeois middle class the number of baptized Jews, of people of mixed "Non-Aryan" descent and of people who were married to "Non-Aryans" increased rapidly. Whereas, there were about 600,000 Jews in Germany proper, the number of non-Jewish "Non-Aryans" of all categories has been estimated by the London *Times* as in excess of 2,-500,000. In Vienna there were 200,000 members of the Jewish community, but at least 500,000 non-Jewish "Non-Aryans". Apart from a small percentage of proletarian Jews recently immigrated from the East, most of these Jews and "Non-Aryans" belonged to the bourgeoisie—often not according to income or wealth but always according to mentality. For they owed their position to the bourgeois tenets and found social equality in the bourgeois class. Only about one-fifteenth of the German bourgeoisie were Jewish, but more than one-quarter were "Non-Aryan" to some extent. In Vienna the Jews accounted for 20 per cent of the bourgeoisie, but Jews and "Non-Aryans" together represented at least 75 per cent. The mixing was confined to the bourgeoisie as the only section of the population which found itself in a common front with the Jews. If to be mixed with the bourgeoisie became the specific distinction of the Jews, to be mixed with Jews became the specific distinction of the bourgeoisie.

This became important when the bourgeoisie attained power after the war. Contrary to Nazi assertions, neither Jewish nor "Non-Aryan" economic wealth and influence increased in the postwar period. On the contrary, the higher estimation of the bourgeois occupations in the postwar society attracted an enormous influx of new, non-Jewish blood into industry, business, and the professions. These newcomers, who before the war would have joined the army or the civil service, took over most of the leading bourgeois positions from the aging Jewish or "Non-Aryan" holders. Postwar Germany did not produce a single Jewish business leader of importance;

whereas, before the war all but a dozen of the leading industrialists and bankers had been Jews, "Non-Aryans," or related to Jews. Jewish wealth and income declined probably twice as fast as the wealth and income of the non-Jewish bourgeoisie. In Vienna, where the Jewish community watched these trends closely, I was shown figures according to which by 1933 the income of the members of the Jewish community had declined by about 60 per cent of the prewar figure, whereas the income of the Gentile upper and middle classes had only fallen by some 30 per cent. Yet the Nazi statement that the Jews had enormously increased their positions and that they held all the power appeared so evident as to be incontrovertible. For, whereas the ruling classes before the war had been free of Jewish blood, the mixture with Jewish blood was the specified distinction of the new ruling class.

When this class failed and when its rule led to the emergence of the demons, it became therefore "rational" to hold the Jews responsible and to personify the demons as Jewish. Such a personification had to proceed on the basis of a racial theory. The persistent allegiance of so many Christians to the tenets of democracy and bourgeois capitalism would have made anti-Semitism pointless unless it could be proved that these Christians were tainted with Jewish blood. Moreover, the racial theory makes it impossible for the individual Jew to escape persecution by baptism, as was always possible in the past. The racial theory therefore invests the Jews with the quality of unalterable viciousness and enmity which fascism needs in its demonic enemies.

In comparison with the Jews, even the Communists are of doubtful value as demonic enemies. For the individual Communist can always recant; but "once a Jew, always a Jew." Once the Jewish race is thus "unmasked" as the demonic force which creates depressions, unemployment, and war, it is logical in a system that seeks its justification in war on others to regard all its members as outlaws and to justify every cruelty and persecution against them. If Jewry is the demonic force that threatens the rational existence of society and of the individual, no *modus vivendi* is possible between the Jewish race and humanity.

Nazi anti-Semitism is therefore due neither to the irreconcilable conflict between the Nordic and the Semitic principle as the Nazis assert, nor to the inherent anti-Semitism of the German people, as is so often said in the outside world. It has been caused precisely by the absence of any distinction, conflict, and strangeness between the German Jews and a large part of the German people—to wit, the liberal middle classes. The Nazis do not persecute the Jews because they remained a foreign body within Germany, but actually because they had become almost completely assimilated and had ceased to be Jews.

It is therefore quite irrelevant what the Jews really are, or what their character, their actions, and their thoughts are. The famous *Protocols of Zion* can be proved a hundred times a clumsy forgery; they must be genuine, as the Jewish conspiracy against Germany must be real. It is irrelevant that the Jews in Czechoslovakia, Poland, Yugoslavia, and Rumania have been for centuries the spearhead of German culture, German trade, and German influence, and that time and again they have saved the German minorities in these countries from extinction. To admit that would mean the self-abandonment of Nazi society and Nazi ideology. It is equally useless to point out that Mr. Roosevelt's name was not originally Rosenfeld; that Stalin, a Georgian, comes from the purest "Aryan" stock in the world and that his father's name was not Levi; or that Lord Baldwin's mother was not the daughter of a Rumanian rabbi. All these lies must remain the official truth in Germany; for the opposition of these men to the principles of Nazism can be explained only by their being Jews. The hundreds of volumes on the Jewish question that have been written since the Nazis came to power—by orthodox Jews, by liberal Jews, by Catholics, Protestants, Marxists, and old-fashioned Liberals—are therefore beside the point. The most profound analysis of the racial, national, and religious characteristics of the Jewish people cannot explain why there has to be racial anti-Semitism in Nazi Germany. It has nothing to do with any qualities of the Jews themselves, but exclusively with what the internal tension in Nazism requires the Jews to look like. For the internal purposes of Nazism, racial anti-Semitism is only a means. The real enemy is not the Jew but the bourgeois order which is fought under the name of the Jew. Nazi anti-Semitism stems from the failure of Nazism to replace the bourgeois order and the bourgeois concept of man with a new constructive concept. And this makes it imperative to denounce bourgeois liberalism and capitalism, yet impossible to resort to class war.

It follows from the logic, inner dynamics, and the purpose of this personification of the demons in all spheres of society that the fight against the invented demonic forces cannot relax. Totalitarian fascism can never be pacified, satisfied, and stabilized. The only way in which it can be made to appear purposeful and in which it can justify itself is the "holy war" against its own demons. There can be no lasting peace and not even a lasting truce between the fascist countries and the democracies. The more the whole economy becomes subordinated to armaments, the more important does it become to make them appear rational. Armaments can only be rationalized and justified by new "grievances" and by new accusations of aggressive intentions against the democracies. There must always be an implacable enemy. The totalitarian countries must always appear insufficiently armed and always violated in some fundamental and vital right or possession.

The same applies to anti-Semitism. The more persecuted and downtrodden Jews and "Non-Aryans" are, the more must further persecution and expropriation appear necessary for the self-assertion and the self-justification of the regime. The very fact that the persecution of the Jews does not lead to the emergence of a new constructive totalitarian ideology must be taken as "proof" that the Jews are really demonic enemies and that their power instead of decreasing has increased through persecution. The Jewish question can never be "finally solved" by Nazism. This applies as much today as it has during all the years since 1933, when the Nazis announced one "final solution" after the other—first full minority rights, then full equality for Jews in business after their exclusion from cultural life, full equality for Jewish war veterans, and so on. It is quite likely that the Nazi officials who announced these stages as "final" acted in good faith; for they themselves hardly understand the function of racial anti-Semitism. They will continue to announce "final solutions." But it is certain that these will go the same way as the earlier ones. If today "half-Jews" are still exempted from some of the anti-Semitic measures, they will be treated as "full Jews" a year from now; and later on it will be the turn of the "quarter-Jews" and then of the "one-eighth Jews." The only thing which the Nazis cannot allow is a real solution. They will therefore probably consent to mass emigration of German Jews only if they have found new Jewish minorities further east as an object of persecution. For they cannot do without the Jews as personified demons and as the irreconcilable enemies of their empire.

To the extent that the problem of self-assertion and self-justification becomes more and more urgent, totalitarianism must invent new personifications of new demons. Racial anti-Semitism, for instance, serves no social purpose outside central and eastern Europe. In western Europe the Gentile bourgeoisie and the Jews have been sharply separated with social intercourse and mixed marriages rigidly limited. This does not mean that there cannot be or that there will not be anti-Semitism accompanying the collapse of the bourgeois order. On the contrary, the Jews who have been emancipated by the bourgeois revolution and who have no other basis for their claim to social equality than the tenets of bourgeois democracy, are especially vulnerable as soon as these tenets no longer appear valid. But to make racial anti-Semitism a vital issue and to hold, for instance, the Jews in France responsible for the French Revolution, would be as socially purposeless as it was socially purposeful in Germany to identify them with the defeat in the war and with Versailles.*

But racial anti-Semitism in France would still be infinitely more intelligible than racial anti-Semitism in Italy. Of all European countries—with the single exception of Scandinavia—Italy has the smallest percentage of Jews. Moreover, the Jews in Italy were as much imbued with the spirit of rabid Italian nationalism—the social movement of middle-class opposition against the old aristocracy, right up to the war—as they were influenced by bourgeois liberalism in Germany. Finally, the personification of the bourgeois spirit in demonic form which Germany achieves by anti-Semitism has been largely achieved in Italy by the campaign against the Freemasons. Because there were no Freemasons left while the bourgeois spirit continued, Mussolini had to adopt racial anti-Semitism. He had to concoct a "proof" of the racial purity of the Italians, who had always justly prided themselves upon their successful assimilation of other racial strains. He had to forbid mixed mar-

* In eastern Europe, on the other hand, especially in Poland, Rumania, Lithuania, and in the western Ukraine which formed part of philo-Semitic medieval Poland, anti-Semitism proves socially even more important than in Germany. Complete elimination of the Jews would eliminate the bourgeoisie altogether in a veritable social revolution. In these precapitalist countries where the indigenous population is still entirely agricultural, whatever there is of a bourgeoisie is Jewish. Although only a small fraction of the Jews are bourgeoisie and most of them live in abject poverty without any property, even the proletarian Jews in these countries represent the "bourgeois" spirit of the society of Economic Man.

riages, which he himself advocated only a few years ago. For fascism needed a new enemy for its "holy war"; it had to create outside hostile forces to explain and to justify its inability to give the noneconomic society of the corporative state a positive social substance.

Similarly, the Nazis forced themselves into a "holy war" against the Catholic Church, although it had been Hitler's sincere intention to avoid repeating Mussolini's mistake in fighting the church, and although the Concordat with Rome had been officially proclaimed the masterpiece of Nazi statesmanship. In fighting the church the Nazis seek to overcome the concept of peace which they are unable to master. Because this concept threatens the validity of their society, they had to give it a demonic personification in the "international" Roman church. The Nazis know very well that a drive against the church is the greatest danger to German unity in view of the deep historical cleavage between Catholics and Protestants. They also know that such a drive can only end in disaster. Nevertheless, they have to undertake it. Otherwise their creed and their society remain without sense, without justification, and without substance. The Italian fascists know equally well that a racial theory is political suicide for any Mediterranean Power. The outside world might be fooled into believing that it will help in the administration of Italy's African colonies, but the Italians know better. Yet all foreknowledge of the dan-

gerous economic and political consequences cannot prevail against the inner logic and the dynamics of totalitarian ideology. The ideological necessity of fascism to
invent "holy wars" proves stronger than all political
intentions and programs and more pressing than all considerations of national economy and of practical politics.

It must be understood that for the convinced Totalitarian the personification of the demons and their persecution and oppression appear not only justified but
alone reasonable. He is genuinely unable to understand
why the outside world does not see the demons. He must
believe that the opposition of the outside world to his
tenets and methods is either conspiracy, hypocrisy,
feeble-mindedness, or madness. For in his eyes it does
not violate reason to see demonic forces in Freemasons
or in Jews or in Catholic priests. On the contrary; otherwise there would be no reason and no justification for
his own society and to his own creed. If the outside world
understands something else by reason, then he has to
reject reason in order to preserve the rationality of his
own world. The more unreasonable the "holy war"
against the demons of his own making appears to others,
the more must it appear to him as the only possible rationalization of the world. This answers the often-asked
question, how a people as little given to hatred as the
Germans could engage in the merciless persecution of
the Jews, or how a people as full of Latin logic as the

Italians could swallow the campaign which made Eden appear personally responsible for every adverse development.

But although a "holy war" appears sensible, it cannot serve as a sufficient substitute for a constructive positive creed. The further the drive against the personified demons proceeds, the less satisfying does it become and the greater must be the disappointment that it does not solve anything. Simultaneously with the increasing acceptance of the "holy war" slogan as alone rational, grows the constant and increasing doubt in its efficacy. Therefore the masses, both in Italy and in Germany, have become not only more afraid of war than the masses in the democracies, but also far more dubious about the merits of arming. The frequent assertion made by shrewd observers that the German masses today are the least anti-Semitic of all people is certainly an exaggeration. But it is doubtless correct that anti-Semitism has become less popular to the degree to which the drive against the Jews has been accelerated.

The nature of totalitarianism and of the belief in it is such, however, that the inner tension can only be met by a further acceleration of the drive against the demons. A creed that exhausts itself in denial can only turn its failure to create a positive satisfaction into additional "proof" that a further denial is necessary, valid, and right. The marked disapproval which the German masses expressed over the looting of Jewish property and the destruction of Jewish hospitals, synagogues, and orphanages was genuine. But equally genuine and almost inevitable was the attempt to overcome the failure of anti-Semitism to furnish the final solution by new and more severe measures against the Jews. The fact that the drive against the Catholic Church is unpopular everywhere in Germany will only lead to its acceleration.

To say that it is the government that forces the stricter anti-Semitic measures or the acceleration of the anti-Catholic drive on the unwilling and silently opposing masses, is a contradiction in itself. No totalitarian regime could do anything against the will of the masses. The absolute and uncontrolled Fuehrer is far more dependent upon their slightest whim than the government of popular democracy. The masses themselves know no other answer than to push on if the totalitarian witch-hunt fails to satisfy their demand for a rational order and a comprehensible society. And the more they push on, the less satisfied do they become. They are caught in a vicious spiral which drives them onward not in spite of, but because of, the demand for a positive creed, which becomes both less answerable and more urgent with every turn.

This failure to create a new order, new values, and a new social creed in the place of the order, the values, and the creed which have collapsed, compels fascism and Nazism to be "totalitarian." Their regime cannot exist unless it asserts that a genuine order, genuine values, and a genuine creed are not only entirely superfluous but that they do not even exist. Totalitarianism must reject the demand made upon every preceding social order in Europe, to justify itself and its authority. It must maintain that the mechanical, external organization of society constitutes its own justification and that it is a social order in itself. Not only must the mere hull of the social fabric be supreme compared to all social substance: the empty mechanical form must also be the supreme social substance itself. *Organization must serve for creed and order.*

One has often ridiculed the old maiden ladies who, when asked about their impressions upon visiting Mussolini's Italy, replied that they did not see any beggars and that the trains ran on time. But their observation comes nearer the essentials of fascism than most of the learned treatises. That the trains run on time, that the beggars have been chased off the main streets, that Italy has the fastest motorships on the southern Atlantic or the widest motor roads—all these purely mechanical details of technical efficiency and organization have come to be regarded as social ends in themselves, regardless of their technical, economic, or military utility. The democracies are deemed inferior not only because they cannot give social equality, but because they cannot mobilize a million men for a mass rally or because they cannot organize uniform applause for their leaders. Free capitalism is not inferior to totalitarian economics because it leads to depressions, but because it has no centralized foreign exchange control. The great historical achievement of Nazism, according to serious Nazi spokesmen, is seen in the outward unification of the various provincial German administrations.

Bourgeois capitalism and Marxist socialism broke down because the mechanist concept of the world and of society collapsed. The only answer which fascism can find is to make the naked mechanism supreme and to glorify it as the final end in itself. The only way which fascism can find to combat the demons of the old order is to invent new demons. Just as the negative character of "holy war" against these self-invented demons can never satisfy the demand for a positive creed, organization qua organization can never satisfy the demand for a new order. But fascism cannot supply a new order. The more insistent the demand for an order becomes, the more must it emphasize organization as the supreme end to which everything must be subordinated. Therefore organization must be "total," and all potential superior ends, that is, all traces and remnants of a real order, must be suppressed.

In the name of organization, fascism must abolish all personal liberty and freedom and destroy all genuine

social units—the family, the youth groups, students'
fraternities, political parties, professional associations.
It must fight all genuine aspirants to an order, whether
their basis is spiritual like that of the churches, economic
like that of the trade-unions, or of the industrialists'
organizations, social like that of the pre-Nazi German,
or the pre-fascist Italian armies, or political like that of
the German monarchists. However spurious their claims,
however weak their following, every one of them disrupts fascist society by its very existence. It is quite
irrelevant whether such social communities are politically pro-fascist, anti-fascist, or as indifferent politically
and socially as a glee club. Fascism can make organization supreme only if it keeps suppressed all potential competition in all spheres. Any real social organism would automatically supersede organization. And
only if organization is accepted as supreme can fascism
accomplish the miracle of restoring the rationality of
society.

As to the efficiency of organization itself, nothing
could be more dangerous than to set it up as an end in
itself. Technically and mechanically, the result must be
overorganization of the most serious type. Planning and
a false precision have been driven so far in Italy as well
as in Germany that a breakdown of one minute cog in
the overcentralized and overorganized machinery of government and business causes the most far-reaching dis-

turbances. The complete abolition of individual decision and discretion on the part of subordinates has made them unable to do anything at all on their own initiative. This has been strikingly illustrated several times in the German railroad organization. Minor divergences from schedule which formerly would have been ironed out without trouble by local officials, have led to long tie-ups of whole districts, as new orders had to be obtained from some central office far from the scene. As long as the system works on schedule, it is a marvel fit to gladden the heart of any efficiency expert; but once there is the slightest disturbance, everything is thrown out of gear.

Another consequence which is just as serious is the inability of any one person to understand and to direct the whole. Everything has become far too complex. It is an open secret in Germany and in Italy that nobody, save perhaps the head of the government itself, knows the full financial status of the country. The Minister of Finance knows the budget, the income from taxes and other revenues, the government loans, etc. But he does not know the financial activities of the hundreds of government agencies with independent borrowing powers. He does not know the financial status of the governing party which competes with the State for the revenues. He does not know the dozens of secret propaganda funds. Moreover, every part of the organization tries to keep its operations secret from all the others; every section tries to enlarge its scope at the others' expense and to become itself the most powerful factor in its field. For if organization is made an end in itself, the struggle for power over the organization becomes necessarily a struggle for power within the organization.

Economically this means that business in the totalitarian states has to pay heavily for wasteful and useless red tape. In Germany these payments are estimated to amount to 25 per cent of industrial costs. Since nobody has any decisive authority save the planning board at the top, every small detail has to be referred to countless conflicting authorities. An everyday matter such as permission to accept an export order requires up to 120 different permits and forms.

Socially the enthronement of organization as supreme has led to the emergence of the organizing bureaucracy as the socially most powerful class. All it does is to organize itself. The emergence of this privileged class of two and a half million supervisors of foreign exchange and raw materials, party secretaries, labor-front and peasant-front organizers, etc., not only presses toward ever increasing overorganization, but also threatens to upset the whole precarious social balance of the fascist noneconomic society.

But the most dangerous consequence for a society which regards the army as its prototype is the grave weakening of military strength. Although a centralized organization appears necessary in modern warfare, it is essential that its subdivisions function independently in the face of the unexpected and not-provided-for. The history of the World War provides a striking example of the danger of overorganization. Germany lost the first battle of the Marne in the fall of 1914 because over-organization and overcentralization had deprived her officers of the power to decide for themselves without sanctions from the commander in chief. The temporary lack of communications between headquarters and the two army corps which rapidly advanced on Paris there-fore led to the panicky decision to retreat. In the far less organized French army, however, a subordinate general himself took the decision to pursue these re-treating corps—against all orders and plans. The dis-astrous consequences for Germany were lessened by the completely unplanned and unprovided-for victory over the Russians staged by Hindenburg and Ludendorff— the two "nonconformists" in the prewar General Staff. But, although organization then enabled Germany to last out for another four years, she never recovered from the disruption of her carefully organized plan for a speedy victory in the West. The Marne was the turning point.

Under fascism, the army and the entire life are even more centralized than Germany's prewar army ever was. Every unexpected development, however small, will be-come an almost unsolvable problem spelling chaos and panic. The entirely futile and pathetic resistance of a few Tyrolean mountain peasants against Germany's occupation of Austria in the spring of 1938 paralyzed a whole army corps for a day or two. It disrupted all supply services in western Austria because the blueprints had not provided for it. In a completely centralized organization which is its own end and its own justification, the blueprint is sacred; when it fails everything fails.

If the economic, social, and military consequences are serious, the metaphysical and ideological weakness of a system that bases itself on organization as a substitute for order and creed is fatal. Organization cannot be accepted as an end in itself. It cannot satisfy the masses; and it does not satisfy them in the totalitarian countries. They are always demanding more—a new substance of society. But the only thing which they can be given is more organization. Every six months a new social order, every one "final," is announced with great pomp and circumstance; a new labor front, a new peasants' corporation, a new ministry, a new final church settlement. Every time this new social order turns out to be nothing but a new organization, serving nobody but itself, organizing nothing but itself. And again, six months later, up comes another white rabbit from the bottomless hat of the planning magician, only to be revealed after a short while as another lifeless mechanical toy.

This inability to produce an order and this inevitable

failure of its substitute, organization, explain the most contradictory, the most puzzling, and at the same time the most important feature of totalitarian society: the form in which the masses believe in it and accept it. Of two observers, of whom the one asserts that the great majority of the people in Germany and Italy are firmly in favor of the regime and the other that they are deeply dissatisfied, one must seemingly be wrong. But both are right at the same time: the masses become the more firmly attached to the regime the more dissatisfied they are.

The key to this contradiction is that the masses have no alternative. To return to bourgeois democracy or to socialism would be returning to a senseless collapsed world ruled by intolerable demons. It is, of course, possible that the masses will be forced to retrograde. But only by compulsion from the outside, for instance after a complete collapse in a disastrous war. Even then such a restoration would be as artificial as it would be short-lived, unreal, and meaningless. There is no return to the old orders once they have collapsed. Their values and concepts, their ideas and their institutions, become unendurable once the routine mind has ceased to accept them as valid. But there are no new values, no new order. Nothing shows this better than the pathetic sterility and the futility of the brave democratic and left-wing underground movements in Italy and Germany.

Not a single one attracts any young or any new members. Not a single one succeeds in developing a program of social organization for the time after the fascist collapse. They are just negative; but the negation of a negation is no positive program. The only underground movement of any influence and importance in Germany is, significantly enough, one that accepts the totalitarian position and only demands a restatement of totalitarian aims: Otto Strasser's "Black Front," which grew out of the Nazi movement itself and only split with Hitler because he was not radical enough. Strasser is a National-Bolshevist in the same sense in which Hitler is a National-Socialist; and he alone of all anti-Nazi leaders knows what he wants.

The masses must have something. They cannot endure the vacuum. Though they are deeply dissatisfied with what totalitarianism has to offer, they cannot get anything else. Therefore totalitarianism must be the valid answer. The less satisfied they are with what it gives, the more must they try to persuade themselves that it is enough. And the more they persuade themselves, the less satisfied must they necessarily become in turn, only to be forced to persuade themselves still further.

This creates the continuous tension under which the masses in the totalitarian countries live. They are deeply unhappy, deeply disappointed, deeply disillusioned. But they must force themselves with all their power to believe in totalitarianism just because they are disillusioned and dissatisfied. What is left to them when they give up the only thing they have? They are like drug addicts who have to take increasing doses of the poison, knowing that it is a poison, but unable to give it up because they must find oblivion and the happiness of dream. That explains the hysteria which grips the masses in every totalitarian meeting, parade, or pageant. They must convince themselves collectively that theirs is the right society. Individually every one of them knows or feels that he has nothing. That your neighbor is enthusiastic becomes a convincing argument for being enthusiastic yourself, even though the neighbor's enthusiasm is equally synthetic.

The most outspoken and most pathetic sufferers of this hysterical and desperate need for self-persuasion are the boys and young men of superior intelligence, education, and feeling whom one finds so often in today's Germany and Italy. They know and feel very well that totalitarianism is suicide for the people and for society. But they fight daily and hourly to convince themselves that it is the ideal society and the creed of the millennium. They pour all their energies, knowledge, and intelligence into this task, which at the bottom of their hearts they know to be futile. Lucky those few who can shut their eyes and accept the outworn creeds and orders of yesterday. Luckier even those very few who can believe in the self-justification of sacrifice and who are ready and eager to lose their lives. But the great majority can neither live in the past nor seek sense in senseless death before they have even begun to live. They must live in the present. That they can achieve only by greater and greater doses of the drug of unconvincing self-conviction and disillusioned enthusiasm.

The intellectual tension of this constant self-persuasion to believe against belief, to trust against evidence, and to cheer spontaneously after careful rehearsal is so great that no amount of self-doping could keep it from snapping. An entity must be found in which the contradiction resolves itself. Since there can be no entity within the realm of reason, it must be found in that of mysticism. No man and no organization can resolve the contradiction between the need for an order and the impossibility of producing one, between the disillusionment over totalitarianism and the need to believe in it. And since the totalitarians have no God, they must invent a Demon, a superman and magician in whom the contradictory becomes one. To be this demon in whom wrong is right, false true, illusion reality, and emptiness substance is the function of the "leader."

The "leader" is human only in the flesh. In the spirit he is beyond human fallibility, beyond human ethics, and beyond human society. He is "always right"; he can never err. His will determines what is good or evil.

His position is outside and beyond society and does not rest upon any social sanction. Only thus can the tension of totalitarian society be made tolerable. Only blind and unquestioning belief in the leader can give the security of conviction which the totalitarian creed itself can never give and yet has to give.

In itself the totalitarian leader-principle is completely foreign to all other totalitarian tenets. To reconcile the glorification of one man with the creed that law and reason are exclusively of the political and social organization for the greater glory of which all individuals exist, is only possible on the basis of abject belief in a mystery. And it is as a mystery in the full theological sense of the word that the leader-principle is treated by the theoreticians of totalitarianism.

The principle is equally different from all forms of one-man rule in the European past. Whether the ruler based his claim upon divine right in a divinely ordered world, upon might of arms, or upon the people's mandate, he always had a social sanction for his rule. The totalitarian dictator has none. His professed accountability to God is an empty phrase, for neither he nor his followers believe in a god. His "mandate from the people" is equally meaningless, for he does not recognize the people's right to select its rulers. The only basis of his claim, the only sanction for his position and power, is that he is above ordinary man. He is a demon in whom the fundamental and irresolvable conflicts of totalitarian society find their solution. His authority is justified as long as he can inspire the masses with the belief which they crave in order to escape despair.

The despair of the masses made in the leader-principle the one spontaneous contribution to the totalitarian creed. No philosopher, no political theorist stood god-father to it. The pseudo-aristocratic leader-theories of Mussolini and Hitler have little in common with fascist reality except the name. Nietzsche's Superman is entirely asocial and anarchist, so that his invocation as the spiritual ancestor of fascism sounds like a bad joke. For the main function of the fascist dictator is to save society by his personal demonic charism. It is no accident that German Protestant farmers generally put Hitler's picture where the picture of Christ used to hang. Nazi sects such as, for instance, the "German Christians" see clearly that their concept of the leader—of human appearance and body but of divine nature—is that of the Messiah, secularized.

"Hitler is always right" and "Mussolini is always right" are the fundamental dogmas of a mystery. Only unquestioning belief in them can make the world and society rational and tolerable, for they alone make possible the necessary belief in totalitarianism. The belief in these dogmas is entirely of the nature of genuine spiritual belief—an experience before and outside the realm of reason which is not susceptible to criticism or discussion.

It is this belief which grips the masses and on which the fascist regimes rest. It is not only the one genuine experience which most of the people have, but for the vast majority it is the only genuine experience which they can have. At the same time it is one which they must have. They must confirm themselves the more in it, the less happy and satisfied they become with totalitarianism.

It is obvious that basing society upon a spiritual belief in the demonic nature of a leader aggravates all the problems of a one-man dictatorship, especially the critical question—what is going to happen after his death. It is possible that this difficulty can be overcome by using the memory of the dead dictator as a potent invocation to blind belief in his successor. But it is not very probable that such an attempt will succeed. Under far more auspicious circumstances Stalin failed to base his rule upon the charism of the dead Lenin, although Lenin died a martyr. Stalin did, however, succeed in substituting himself as charismatic leader. Unless the successor to the fascist dictator is able to do the same he will be overthrown.

Since there cannot be any legitimate order of succession to charismatic leadership, preparations and speculations as to the succession necessarily occupy the central place in all internal developments. In Germany the intrigues between the several factions of potential "crown princes" reach down to the most subordinate local official. Many, if not all, of the continuous feuds within the Nazi administration which undoubtedly weaken the regime seriously, have no other foundation than personal enmity and jealousy between potential pretenders to the succession. Yet nothing appears destined to destroy the whole basis of belief in the leader-principle quicker than a fight for the succession. Mussolini sought, therefore, to prevent the emergence of a "crown prince." But he could only rid himself of potential successors and of their intrigues by keeping all but mediocrities away from the seat of power. Starace, Balbo, Suvich, De Bono, and many less important men were retired or politely deported as soon as they assumed an independent status. Since there has to be somebody with first-class administrative experience, lest the power fall back at once into the hands of the violently anti-fascist royal family, Mussolini had to groom the one senior official whose insignificance seemed sufficient guarantee against the temptation to intrigue: Ciano. To give him a legitimate claim over the others he was married to Mussolini's daughter. But unless Ciano should suddenly develop a charismatic claim of his own to leadership—which does not appear likely—he will be unable to carry on. If he is not destroyed in the fight for the succession, he will at best be able to retire with dignity like Cromwell's son.

In addition the leader-principle fails as a political and ideological solution of the totalitarian problem. It can resolve the inner totalitarian conflict only by increasing the intellectual and nervous tension. Nobody can live all the time in the atmosphere of a revivalist meeting; but this atmosphere must be maintained in order to maintain totalitarianism. This tension must become increasingly marked as the "totalitarianizing" of society proceeds. Finally it will reach a point where the slightest doubt in the leader is disastrous. The more necessary it becomes for the leader to be accepted as infallible, the more difficult will it be for him to maintain the belief that he is always right; accordingly, the more vulnerable he and the regime become. For the belief in the demonic nature of a fellow man must assert itself anew every day; the miracle must be repeated with increasing success and at decreasing intervals. The belief in the miracle becomes more feverish all the time. The more the masses need the belief in the leader, the more they feel the strain which this belief imposes and its danger of sudden collapse.

This collapse will come as soon as there is an alternative to the belief in the demonic nature of the leader, that is, as soon as there is a new order and a new creed. But —and that is the mainspring of totalitarian successes and strength—it cannot come otherwise. There can be no doubt that the masses in their great majority will continue to worship their self-invented demon out of sheer despair as long as the only alternative is the vacuum.

But there can equally be no doubt that 99 per cent of the German or of the Italian people would at once rally round any new order which would provide a rational society and a rational world in which the individual would again have a rational place and a rational function. This was strikingly shown during the last desperate and courageous attempt of Dr. Schuschnigg, Austria's last chancellor, to find a new social basis and a new order in March, 1938. Schuschnigg's attempt was really based on nothing but personal courage and on an appeal to the courage of the masses. It failed as pathetically to give a new idea and a new order as all his former attempts at a "Catholic corporate state" had failed. There was no possible basis, and there had been none in Austria ever since capitalist democracy and socialism had collapsed together in 1927. But the attempt alone, the mere hope—though futile—that there could be a new order, had such sudden and profound effect upon the masses throughout Germany that Hitler would have been forced to destroy Austria by armed invasion even if he had not already decided to do so. It is very probable that Hitler knew that there was no risk involved, but he would have had to risk even a major war. Otherwise the Nazi regime would have collapsed. In the Aus-

trian Tyrol, in Bavaria, and in the German Southwest
—strongholds of religious Nazism—even old party members had already begun to waver. But as soon as the invasion into Austria destroyed the hope of an alternative, the totalitarian belief in Hitler recovered at once. And the Austrian masses who until then had still believed in a way out, were forced by their despair to turn Nazi themselves. This explains the rapid conversion, the lack of even passive resistance, and the outbreak of Nazi terror in its worst form in formerly anti-Nazi Vienna, which have puzzled all outside observers.

The totalitarian revolution is clearly not the beginning of a new order but the result of the total collapse of the old. It is not a miracle, but a mirage which will dissolve as soon as a new order, a new concept of man, appear. Fascism can only deny the concept of Economic Man which has broken down. It cannot create the new concept which should take its place. But unless a new order and new concept based upon the European values of freedom and equality can be found, Europe and the Occident are doomed.

The form which the totalitarian revolution has been taking indicates in itself that such an order will eventually arrive. That the masses substitute organization for order when they cannot have a real order, that they worship a demon when they have no God to worship and no concept of man to respect, shows by its very intensity that they must have an order, a creed, and a rational concept of man. The more fervently they turn fascist, the more feverishly do they search for something else. And the more eagerly will they embrace the new order when it appears. Armaments, the totalitarian organization of society, the suppression of freedom and liberties, the persecution of the Jews, and the war against religion are all signs of weakness, not of strength. They have their roots in blackest, unfathomable despair. The more desperate the masses become, the more strongly entrenched will totalitarianism appear to be. The further they push on the totalitarian road, the greater will be their despair. As soon as they are offered an alternative—but no sooner—the whole totalitarian magic will vanish like a nightmare.

Nothing the totalitarians can do to fortify their power will be the slightest protection against the sweep of a new order which will again give the masses a positive creed instead of a gospel of pure negation; which will again affirm the validity of life and of society instead of preaching senseless sacrifice; which will again give man dignity and value instead of denying his very existence. Not even the totalitarian education which seizes the youngest infants, and which has been regarded generally as the greatest danger to civilization, will alter the situation in the least. The youth of a country may be regimented for a positive idea and order. They can only be kept regimented for the negative and for the sake of organization as long as there is no alternative. Children can be educated to think exclusively in one direction, but they cannot successfully be educated not to think at all.

This confidence in the ultimate emergence of a new order gains support if our times are viewed in historical perspective, that is, from the point of view of the continuity of Occidental history. For ours is not the first time in which this continuity has been broken. Twice before, in the thirteenth century and in the sixteenth, European order collapsed. Neither a continuation nor any new order were visible or apparent at the time. In both cases the collapse was, as today, caused by the disintegration of the belief in one concept of man: in the thirteenth century in that of Spiritual Man, in the sixteenth century in that of Intellectual Man. Both concepts had disintegrated because it was proved that the society based upon them could not realize freedom and equality in the sphere which it regarded as alone socially constitutive. The societies based upon them collapsed, as today, when they had apparently approached their perfection—the Holy Roman Empire of the early Middle Ages, the Society of Saints of the Puritan reformers.

The parallel can even be extended to details. For what Marxism was to the society of Economic Man, Calvinism was to that of Intellectual Man: the final, messianic exaggeration of its creed. In both, the belief in the attainability of freedom and equality could only be maintained by sacrificing actual freedom. The doctrine of determination through predestination in Calvinism is parallel to that of determination through the class situation in Marxism. Both abolished actual freedom in existing society in order to maintain the belief in the reality and imminence of freedom in the coming society. And both collapsed as orders when it was proved that the only society which they could realize was an unfree society. As today, the transitory period between the collapse of the old and the emergence of the new order was one of chaos, panic, witch-hunts, and "totalitarianism." There also was the belief that the end of the Occident had come and that there could be no new development. But suddenly—apparently out of nowhere—the new order appeared, and the nightmare vanished as if it had never existed. Dante thought that everything worth living for had disappeared with the last Ghibelline emperors; and yet he himself fathered the sudden blossoming of the Renaissance only one generation later. There was nothing but despair when Kepler died in the turmoil of the Thirty Years' War, amidst witch-hunts and the terrors of the Inquisition; but at that time Descartes and the great English political philosophers were already laying the foundations for the new society of Economic Man and for a new order.

The new society which will ultimately arise out of the collapse of the society of Economic Man will again try to realize freedom and equality. Though we do not yet know which sphere will become socially constitutive in the order of the future, we do know that it will not be the economic sphere, which has ceased to be valid. This means that the new order will be able to realize economic equality. For if every European order by virtue of its foundation on the Christian basis seeks to realize freedom and equality, it also seeks this realization in that sphere which it holds to be socially constitutive. Freedom and equality cannot be realized, they can only be promised in that sphere. Their realization in one sphere becomes possible only after a new sphere has become socially constitutive. Thus, religious freedom and religious equality could only be realized after the spiritual sphere had been abandoned as the basis of society. The political equality of formal democracy became possible only after the economic had become the basis of social distinction and satisfaction. Economic equality will equally become possible when it has ceased to be socially all-important and when freedom and equality in a new sphere will be the promise of a new order.

To strive always after the unattainable freedom and the unattainable equality has been the driving force of Occidental history. Whether in the process we have progressed from a lower to a higher sphere, or whether we have been continuously declining, the dynamics and the messianic character of our basis has given us a continuous development, whereas all other civilizations have been stationary. It has also given us the inner ideological power to master the world. Though today this mastership seems to be attacked with weapons which we furnished ourselves, this attack from the outside will collapse as soon as we can find a new valid order.

But the dynamic character of our history, which is all our strength, is also our weakness; for it makes periods of transition like the present one inevitable. Yet that today the European masses flee into the black magic of totalitarianism rather than tolerate a world without order and a society without meaning, only shows that the force that is Europe is still alive.

CHAPTER EIGHT

THE FUTURE:
EAST AGAINST WEST?

THE Western democracies have to realize that totalitarian fascism cannot be overcome by socialism, by capitalist democracy, or by a combination of both. It can only be overcome by a new noneconomic concept of a free and equal society. The fascist countries might be destroyed; they might be reduced to anarchy. But neither capitalism nor socialism can be restored thereby. On the contrary, the Western European democracies themselves will be forced into totalitarianism unless they produce a noneconomic society striving for the freedom and the equality of the individual.

Both the Left and the Right in the democracies have hitherto refused to admit that there is only the alternative between totalitarianism and the new society. Their search for a third possibility which would make possible the maintenance of freedom on the basis of the society of Economic Man resulted, in the field of practical politics, in the expectation of a war between Russia and Germany. It is only through such a war that a totalitarian attack against the West can be prevented. The West could not survive such an attack without either adopting fascism itself or evolving an alternative noneconomic society of freedom and equality. A Russo-German war alone would save the West from being drawn into a general conflagration; such a war is therefore the only way to maintain the society of Economic Man; therefore such a war must be inevitable.

The responsibility for this idea lies with the European Left Wing parties. Their idea of a "united front" between the democracies and "democratic" Russia and their contention that such an alliance would usher in perfect democratic socialism have done greater harm than all other political mistakes of the past twenty years. The proclamation of an "irreconcilable conflict" between Russia and Germany is directly responsible for the pro-fascist sentiment among the European Right Wing parties which is based upon the belief that fascism as an antagonist to communism must be procapitalist, and therefore fundamentally beneficial. Those German businessmen and industrialists, who, lured by the denunciation of fascism as antisocialist, concluded that it must be procapitalist, have since learned better. But, whereas originally the Right in France and in England favored resistance to fascism, the slogan of the inevitable Russo-German war has made a large section favor the fascist advance, so that "both monsters devour each other."

Upon this conviction the entire policy of "appeasement" has been based; to bring the conflict nearer by driving Germany to the East, Czechoslovakia was sacrificed.

Actually, this expectation of a Russo-German war was never much more than wishful thinking. Unless an unforeseeable accident intervenes, there will be no war between Germany and Russia. If there is no war, there must eventually be an alliance of these two Powers against the West. The Left has already learned that the "united front" idea can neither prevent a general war nor stem the fascist tide. And when the Right is shaken out of its complacent belief that there must be war between Germany and Russia, the European democracies will have no program and no policies whatsoever. Actually, the specter of the Russo-German alliance is already the nightmare of every European government, however much they protest their belief in the inevitability of a Russo-German war. And what is only a nightmare today may be reality tomorrow.

The two regimes will have to come together because they are similar ideologically and socially. That the European Left has not dared to admit this is understandable. By conceding that Soviet Russia is as fascist a state as Germany, they would have conceded that socialism must fail and would have abandoned themselves. Yet they have not gained anything by shutting their eyes. On the contrary, their very impotence stems from this inability to admit reality. As for the Right Wing parties, they know that Russia is fundamentally similar to Germany. Their refusal to draw the conclusions, and their insistence that the two must go to war is, therefore, all the more unpardonable. It can only be explained—though not excused—by their despair, which makes them hope for a miracle.

As far as Germany is concerned, she is becoming more totalitarian every day. That means that the possibility of a lasting peace with the West becomes more and more remote. The more totalitarian Germany becomes, the greater becomes the necessity to oppose both democracy and the democracies as demonic enemies. However much German political leaders might want friendship with England, the inherent dynamics and necessities of their totalitarian state will prove stronger than their intentions. If England is not the enemy, France is; and if neither of them, then the United States. For the continued existence of the democracies is the gravest danger to the internal stability of the totalitarian regime. The more concessions the democracies make, the more certain must it appear to Nazism that lasting peace with them is impossible and that the enemy is in the West.

This conviction will be correct: the enemy of totalitarian Nazism is not in the East. It is not Russian communism. The complete collapse of the belief in the attainability of freedom and equality through Marxist socialism has forced Russia to travel the same road toward a totalitarian, purely negative, noneconomic society of unfreedom and inequality which Germany has been following. Not that communism and fascism are essentially the same. Fascism is the stage reached after communism has been proved an illusion. And it has been proved as much of an illusion in Stalinist Russia as it was proved an illusion in pre-Hitler Germany. Communism in anything but name was abandoned in Russia when the Five-Year Plan was substituted for the New Economic Policy (NEP) after Lenin's death. Under NEP there was still the hope of a realization of the free socialist society. Since the First Five-Year Plan it has become increasingly obvious that Marxist socialism can only lead to an even greater inequality; to the complete loss of freedom and to the emergence of a hereditary caste of officials as ruling class. During the last few years Russia has therefore been forced to adopt one purely totalitarian and fascist principle after the other; not, it must be emphasized, because of a "Stalinist conspiracy," but because there was no other possibility. As in Germany, the "noneconomic society" has been initiated. Gradually all other objectives and the entire social structure have been subordinated to an armament drive, the main justification for which is as social as it is in Germany. In Russia too, the regime has come to be dependent for its self-justification and self-rationalization upon the invention of fictitious enemies within and without. And since the purge started, Russia has been living in the same atmosphere of "holy war" against self-invented demons as the fascist countries. The extent to which Russia prepares herself ideologically for this alliance can be seen in her growing emphasis upon the purely negative glorification of organization as an end in itself, and in the elevation of Stalin to the rank of demonic "leader" who can never be wrong. As in Germany, these two tenets have become the only substance of the Russian creed. For both countries the real enemy is the West, with its ideal of freedom, its economic basis of society, and its remnants of the very order which both Germany and Russia deny, refute, and fight.

The fundamental social and ideological dynamic of a revolution is always decisive, both internally and externally. Everything else—economic, military, or political factors—becomes subordinated; these can be supreme or independent only in a static society. Indeed, it is probably the most marked characteristic of a real revolutionary change in the fundamental structure of society that the inner social and ideological dynamic is supreme and decisive. The Russo-German alliance would have to be expected even if all other considerations should speak against it. The inner necessity will press toward it, just as it forced England, Prussia, Austria, and Russia to form an alliance against revolutionary France in 1791, or the new-born United States to sympathize with the French Republic and to wage war in 1812 on the side of Napoleon instead of against him. But in addition to the ideological basis, the Russo-German alliance would have a solid economic and military foundation. In fact, it would be the only means by which both countries could overcome their economic and military difficulties.

Economically, only through an alliance with Russia can Germany solve her one problem: the dependence on imports of raw materials from the world markets which forces her to accelerate dangerously the reduction of consumption. The advisability of such an alliance should be greatly increased by the economic consequences of Germany's Balkan campaign. Control of the Balkans and of the raw materials of southeastern Europe will in all probability not diminish but increase Germany's import troubles. It is correct that the Balkans contain large raw material resources, though their wealth is generally exaggerated. But the Balkans are not new colonial territory. They are the most heavily overpopulated part of Europe, though they show only an average density of population in the usual statistics. Since there are, however, no large cities in southeastern Europe, this average figure conceals an enormous overcrowding on the land. In no Balkan country is the density of the agricultural population less than twice that of Germany. Also, contrary to general opinion, much of the Balkan soil is extremely poor. Not even a complete land reform in Hungary and Rumania—the only two Balkan countries with large estates—would produce enough land for the landless peasants. Today 80 per cent of the Hungarian peasants have not enough land to grow their own extremely low foodstuff requirements; a complete land reform would still leave two-thirds of the peasants as poorly off as they are today. And the average size of the Balkan farm could not be increased at all above its present three to four acres. Hence, the Balkans do not offer any possibility of settling German farmers.

Germany's conquest of the Balkans depends upon her winning the land-starved and exploited peasants who constitute 90 per cent of the population of all Balkan countries. They must be promised that they shall benefit by German rule through a higher standard of living. The Nazis are fully aware of this; their entire propaganda in the Balkans is directed toward mobilizing the latent forces of peasant revolt against the present Balkan rulers. The Nazis are also fully aware that they can only hope to hold the Balkans and to keep open the access to their raw material reserves in case of war or of a crisis in Germany, if they fulfill at least part of their promises to the peasants. It will therefore be necessary for Germany to give those peasants economic benefits. If these benefits come out of German surpluses, a further reduction in the German internal consumption will be necessary. If they come out of the production of the Balkan countries themselves, there will be a decrease in the quantity of raw materials available for export to Germany. In either case there will be no benefits for Germany. She can force a non-Nazi government of Yugoslavia to take German aspirin in payment for the Yugoslav wheat and the Yugoslav copper ore; it can only be to her advantage if the Yugoslav population, who are offered aspirin instead of the clothes they need, blame their own government for the lack of textiles. But if this government should be Nazi-appointed and a vassal of Berlin, the Nazis cannot risk such discontent. They must offer real goods and a real increase in the standard of living of the masses as the price of military and political overlordship.

This expectation is borne out by the experience which Germany had during the World War when she also dominated the Balkans, including even the Ukraine. Then she could only maintain her hold over the conquered territory by giving the natives a larger share of their own products. Germany therefore, not only did not derive any relief of her own foodstuff and raw material problems, but actually had to help the occupied territories out of her own meager resources.

It is, of course, possible that in the distant future German investments in Balkan industries will bear fruit in the form of greater supplies of raw materials. But for many years an increase in the production of the Balkan countries will be accompanied by a decrease of the exportable surplus. A few German industrialists and bankers might benefit immediately in the form of wind-fall profits, though it is more than likely that profits of this nature will be reserved for the government, as they are in conquered Austria and in the Sudeten territory. But from the point of view of the German economy as a whole, the domination of southeastern Europe should result in a net outlay of capital on which there will be no return for a long time to come, just as Austria and the Sudeten territory require subsidies and investments of capital and goods without promising any return.

Control of the Balkans, therefore, would not solve or even mitigate the German economic problem. But a close economic connection with Russia would meet with none of the economic difficulties encountered in the Balkans. On the contrary, it would altogether solve the economic problem of totalitarianism in Germany. With the sole exception of the Ukraine, Russia is agriculturally under-populated. She has good soil on the average, and her raw material resources are enormous. In the empty plains of Siberia she offers ample scope for the building-up of agricultural enterprises on an industrial, labor-saving, mass-production basis. Finally, though she has laid the foundation for an industry, her lack of capital and the political and physical obstacles against further reduction of consumption will make it difficult if not impossible to utilize this industry without outside help. But industrial production could increase sharply if the necessary capital becomes available. Thus, while the Russian farm population will also have to be given an increased standard of living, production in Russia should increase faster than consumption if new capital is invested. Russia, being sparsely populated but potentially very rich, promises to yield increasing returns; whereas the Balkans, which are overpopulated though poor, could only yield sharply decreasing returns. And Russia needs just those goods of which Germany has a surplus. She needs high-grade mass-production machinery, which to build requires practically no raw materials, but a great amount of technical and engineering skill. She needs an efficient system of transportation and of distribution, which again is a matter of ability and experience rather than of material investments. These services and investments would be of such importance to Russia that she could pay for them many times more than the world-market price, and in the very raw materials which Germany needs.

Theoretically it might appear possible for Russia to obtain the necessary assistance from the democracies, just as it might appear theoretically possible for Germany to solve her economic problems by returning to free capitalism. But it is impossible for either country to obtain the necessary capital from a capitalist country without abandoning her social and political system. A totalitarian social and political society must also have complete economic totalitarianism. The slightest exception to the complete control and to the complete subordination of economic activities to noneconomic objectives disrupts and endangers totalitarian society. The Russians learned this from the "foreign concessions" of the late twenties; though these islands of capitalist enterprise were strictly isolated from the noneconomic society and though they were under complete control, their very existence contaminated the whole body economic. They had to be abolished in spite of their enormous economic usefulness. The political and social realities of totalitarianism forbid close economic collaboration with any country which has not a totalitarian social and political structure. And Russia and Germany will therefore be driven together in their search for outside economic assistance.

Whereas Germany would derive greater economic benefits from an alliance, Russia would be the main beneficiary from the military point of view. The Soviets cannot fight a war on two fronts. The Soviet Far Eastern provinces can be defended against a first-rate Asiatic Power only if the whole might of Russia can be thrown to the Far East. Otherwise this undeveloped, underpopulated, and underfed territory will be overrun. The same applies to the western frontier. Next to Vladivostok, the Ukraine is Russia's most vulnerable spot. The Ukrainians have always resisted Russian domination. They are acutely nationalist, and they are by no means reconciled to the Bolshevik land policy which they—prosperous individual peasants for a long time before the war—regard as a Russian-imposed expropriation in favor of a non-Ukrainian ruling class in the Russian towns. If Russia had to fight in the east and in the west at the same time, the Ukraine would be very difficult to hold; but if there is war only on the western front, the Ukraine is almost impregnable.

It was on these considerations that Russia based her "united front" policy between 1933 and 1938. The close contact with the League of Nations, the collaboration with the western democracies, and the acceptance of collective security were from the Russian point of view nothing but attempts to protect Russia's western flank against German aggression in order to ensure freedom of action in the Far East. After the breakdown of this policy it has become abundantly clear that Russia cannot expect any help from the West against an attack. The Chamberlain government in England even hopes for such an attack; it certainly does not intend to divert Germany from a head-on drive against Russia. Russia must therefore choose whether she wants to make peace with the potential aggressor in the East or with the one in the West. It seems almost impossible that she will succeed in obtaining a lasting agreement in the Far East, if for no other reason than because the Chinese, whose trend of emigration and commercial expansion has been into Soviet territory these last ten years, are potentially no less dangerous than the Japanese. Russia must therefore try to come to terms with Germany.

Germany's position is only slightly better. She too cannot fight a two-frontiers war; if the German General Staff learned one lesson in the World War, this is it. Regardless of what hopes the British and French governments entertain, the German eastward advance will make a permanent agreement with the Western countries impossible. Even if Germany should really want the Ukraine, her advance toward this goal would be an attack upon the French and the British empires, especially upon the latter. It would threaten the whole eastern Mediterranean, Asia Minor, and the Middle East—not to mention the Arab world. Whereas today more than ever before the British Empire's frontier is at the Dardanelles. Germany could do nothing to allay this suspicion that she really wants to obtain control of the eastern Mediterranean; for "Berlin to Baghdad" is as intelligent and intelligible a concept of German policy as "Berlin to Kiev" is an absurdity in view of the overpopulation of the Ukraine. In her drive to the East, Germany would be unable to rely upon British and French neutrality. From the military point of view it must, therefore, be imperative to come to an agreement with Russia whereby the whole Near East would automatically fall to their joint domination regardless of British and French opposition.

The only doubt whether the internal dynamic of the German and of the Russian revolution will really lead to the alliance, arises from obstacles in the persons and in the convictions of the two leaders. In Russia this obstacle is a very minor one. Stalin has undoubtedly taken into account all along the possibility of an accord with Germany. Up to 1935 he maintained excellent German-Russian relations. Until that time German military and aviation schools were kept on Russian soil, and the economic relations between the two countries remained extremely close. And in his purge Stalin took good care to "liquidate" not only the advocates of an alliance with Germany, like the German-trained General Staff, but also the Old Bolsheviks who advocated the "inevitable war" against Germany. Thus the purge gave Stalin a free hand in the matter of foreign politics and enabled him to decide for or against Germany without regard to communist slogans. At first he seemed to lean toward deciding against Germany; up till Munich he followed the anti-German policy—Litvinoff's "collective security" and "united front" ideas. But by now he has learned that these concepts were illusions. His announcement that

Russia will now concentrate upon her "Asiatic mission" can only signify that he contemplates peace in the West, which must sooner or later lead to an agreement with Germany. In addition—this, at least, is the opinion of the shrewdest observers in Germany—the threat of a revolt against him which has been growing ever since the purge, will force him to seek support in the only quarter where he can get it; namely, in Germany. And if there should be a successful revolt against his regime, the new masters would undoubtedly have to make peace with Germany, not only to strengthen their own regime but also in order to obtain a slogan to justify their claim that they bring something new.

Far greater appears to be the obstacle presented by the personal convictions of Hitler. Hitler is still under the spell of the doctrines of Rosenberg, the "spiritual adviser" of the Nazi party. Rosenberg, who was born in prewar Russia and who was an officer in the Czar's army, hates the present regime in Moscow not only for political but for personal reasons. He has been preaching the conquest of the Ukraine which most other leaders in the Nazi party oppose since it is only too well known that the Ukraine is overpopulated. The whole anti-Communism is Rosenberg's who sees in the delivery of Russia from Russian rule—which he regards as Asiatic—and in her restoration to Teutonic rule, the great mission of Nazism. Hitler has been his faithful pupil.

But this argument is inconclusive. In the first place, no revolutionary "leader" has ever been able to oppose the inner dynamic of the revolution which he imagines himself to lead. Danton and Robespierre no less than Trotsky were destroyed as soon as they really attempted to lead by opposing the natural trend of the forces of the revolution. Hitler too would be destroyed if he tried to arrive at a lasting agreement with the West and to wage war against the East. But there is no reason to expect that Hitler will try to oppose the trend. His very leadership and his successes are due to his ability to adapt himself and his theories to every change in the conditions. He signed an agreement with Poland within one year after he came to power, although he had always preached war against the Poles. He accepted social and economic totalitarianism even to the point where it begins to imply the adoption of collective farming, though he had always preached economic liberalism and war on monopolies. He renounced his original condemnation of the prewar drive for colonies and thereby implicitly the whole basis of his policy of friendship with the democracies. Russia would probably only have to make minor concessions such as the dropping of the world revolution —which anyhow has ceased to have any meaning for the Russian masses—and the adoption of anti-Semitism— which would not entail a very radical departure from

the Russian practice of the last years—in order to appear
as an acceptable ally to Hitler.

It is, therefore, of the greatest importance that the
real power in Germany is shifting more and more into
the hands of the one group which opposes any lasting
peace with the West, as it regards the totalitarian world
revolution as the supreme end. This group, which might
be called "Goering's Brain Trust" consists of men like
General Milch, the Chief of Staff of the Airforce; General Loeb, the head of the Four-Year Plan, and Dr. Funk,
Minister of Economics and Economic Dictator of Germany. These men have steadily forced complete state control on German business. They have crowded out, one
after the other, their opponents in business, in the army
command, and in the party. Dr. Schacht was driven out
by them; the head of the Labor Front, Dr. Ley—leader
of anticommunism in the party—has been subordinated
to them; as well as the Minister of Agriculture, Dr.
Darré—a romantic "populist"; and the Minister of
Finance, Count Schwerin—a conservative of the old
school. They forced the retirement of the army High
Command, which opposed totalitarianism and which was
supported by Hitler. Daily they are becoming not only
more powerful but also more indispensable.

These men, with their subordinates, pupils, and adherents, may all be excellent Nazis. But, in the first
place, they believe more in the totalitarian noneconomic

society and in the totalitarian world revolution than in any nationalist or racial tenets of Nazism. They probably know that they need Hitler; but they regard him as a useful tool and as a first-class mass leader rather than as a semi-god. They accept anti-Semitism as an excellent means for destroying the German bourgeoisie, but they see in it nothing else and are little interested in the "Nordic man." After all, Goering's Four-Year Plan organization is the only place in Germany where people of known Jewish or partly Jewish descent are still allowed to hold high office.

Even more significant than all this is the fact that these "confirmed totalitarians" come almost without exception from the school of Walther Rathenau—Jew, Left Wing democrat, Germany's raw material dictator during the war, and assassinated by the Nazis while Foreign Minister—who was the first to preach totalitarian economics. Rathenau did not foresee that totalitarian economics would lead to fascism; on the contrary, he saw in them the final step toward freedom and equality. But he also saw that only under a close alliance with Russia could Germany have a planned economy of state monopoly. He therefore signed, in 1923, the famous Rapallo Treaty with the Soviets which became the basis of the close German-Russian relationship during the Weimar Republic. It seems hardly possible that his pupils—and some of the present members of Goering's Brain Trust were among his closest collaborators—have forgotten what they learned from him. There is definite evidence that these men, who more and more become the real rulers of German destiny, have been counting upon an agreement with Russia all the time, if not as the only choice, at least as the only alternative for Germany.

From every angle the alliance between Germany and Russia seems to be almost unavoidable. Only a war within the very near future could prevent it—1940 might perhaps be considered the latest date. If it should be delayed beyond that time the two countries would inevitably drift closer and closer. It may take two, five, or ten years before the two totalitarian Powers come to a definite understanding. They may arrive at an agreement by partitioning Poland or by driving Italy and Great Britain out of the eastern Mediterranean. Perhaps the alliance will be based upon a pseudo-autonomy for the Ukraine, as the Ukrainians are the only major nation in Europe who have not yet been united in a national state of their own. Their national independence would therefore be a logical and appropriate symbol that nationalism has exhausted itself as the driving dynamic force of Europe and that the social revolution of totalitarianism has become the sole issue.

But all this is comparatively immaterial. Of paramount importance is the fact that the West has to be prepared for the attack of the East, and that this attack will decide the future of Europe. This future will not be primarily dependent upon the military outcome of the war. Europe would still be lost to totalitarianism if the West could only win by going fascist itself. Besides, victory in such a decisive war always falls to him who is morally and socially stronger even if he should be weaker in the field. And a western Europe that has adopted totalitarianism for the sake of fighting totalitarianism would be morally and socially weaker than those who adhere to totalitarian fascism for its own sake.

Should totalitarianism win the war, Europe would undergo a long period of darkness and despair just like the "totalitarian" periods in the thirteenth and sixteenth centuries when there had also been a complete collapse of the preceding European orders. Totalitarianism would eventually overcome itself, and a new order based upon freedom and equality would eventually emerge from the period of totalitarian darkness. Even today, under the avalanche of totalitarian oppression, the individual, whose very existence is denied by fascism, seeks new resources of freedom and a new sphere of independence within himself. Politically impotent as the opposition of the churches has been against the totalitarian attack on the freedom of conscience, "personal religion" has become the refuge of many of the best minds in Germany and Italy. Parallel with it a New Humanism has made its appearance—mainly among the very young, who, ac-

cording to official doctrine, should be completely organized and regimented along totalitarian lines. These
returns to the perennial intellectual and spiritual values
of the European inheritance are not in themselves socially effective, creative, or productive. They are nothing
but desperate attempts to find a sphere of individual
existence and of individual freedom by resignation from
society. But out of a similar resignation of the scholars
of the thirteenth century who retired to their study in
conscious abandonment of their function in society
emerged the Renaissance concept of freedom and the
society of Intellectual Man. Similarly, the concept of
freedom of the bourgeois society of Economic Man grew
out of the conscious social resignation of the "saints" and
of the Quakers. Today we are witnessing the same phenomenon; again it should—eventually—lead to a regeneration. In his self-imposed resignation from society
the individual, freed from the limitations of the concept
of Economic Man, will produce a new, noneconomic, social substance which he will endow with freedom.

But we cannot look upon this prospect with the com-
placency with which the historian of today views the
Thirty Years' War. We must try to develop the other
alternative: the development of a new, free and equal
noneconomic society on the foundation and from the
premises of our existing economic society. If we succeed in this task we need not fear the attack from the

East. For then war would again appear rational and therefore tolerable to the West, as it would be fought for positive values instead of just against something negative. And victory would inevitably fall to the protagonists of the new order.

Physical armaments, however necessary, are not the right means to realize this new society on which alone rest all hopes for successful resistance to the totalitarian onslaught. On the contrary, they constitute in themselves a grave danger, because the subordination of all economic production to armaments and to industrial defense implies the glorification of armaments as a social end, and threatens therefore to establish fascism "by economic default." It is furthermore more than probable that the military are again, as usual, preparing for the last war instead of for the next one. This is perhaps as inevitable in a profession that has nothing but past experience to go on, as it is for the economist always to prepare for the last depression and for the Stock Exchange speculator always to buy the favorites of the last boom. But recognition of this situation should instill a healthy skepticism about any attempt to prepare for the war against totalitarianism by simulating the "total armament" of the totalitarians, which is based primarily upon social, not upon military, considerations.

The only real resistance to the totalitarian onslaught would be to release new basic forces in our own society.

There is no way to produce at will such new forces; for there is no short cut to a new order. How little we know whether such forces even exist underneath the surface is shown by the example of England during the French Revolution. In the years immediately before, England seemed in complete collapse. She had just lost her colonial empire overseas. Her society was as corrupt as her parliament and her government. The monarchy was hated by all classes. The lower classes were in open revolt against the beginning industrial revolution. Industry and trade were on the verge of bankruptcy. Everybody expected the revolution to break out in England at once, except Burke alone, who saw the inner strength beneath all this decay; but he was regarded as a fool by the defeatist majority of all classes. Prussia, on the other hand, seemed at the height of internal strength after the victorious wars and the assiduous industrial policy of Frederick the Great. Yet Prussia collapsed at once like a house of cards, whereas England alone of all European societies stood firm. In the terrible twenty years of the Napoleonic wars she developed the new society of the nineteenth century in historical continuity from that of the eighteenth century. This made England the leading World Power for the next hundred years, made her an example for all the rest of Europe, and provided the basis for the undreamt-of economic and territorial expansion of the nineteenth century. No doubt Napoleon's empire would have fallen to pieces sooner or later, even if the English had not resisted but had collapsed socially and morally. But without the development of the new basic forces of bourgeois democracy by England, Europe would probably have become—after Napoleon's death or fall—the football of his marshals, the theater of endless wars, of impoverishment, of misery, and of brutal persecution for another generation.

We do not know whether such strong, vital forces of a new order are hidden underneath our society, and whether they will be brought out by the terrible ordeal of war. But we can at least prepare our defenses in such a way as not to hinder them. The western European democracies can at least try to make it possible for rigid economic control of modern warfare to be imposed without complete loss of personal freedom. Although they can produce a new order at will as little as they can restore the validity and rationality of capitalism and socialism, they can and should strengthen the dignity and security of the individual in economic society in such a way as to re-endow freedom with some meaning.

It must be clearly recognized that in such an attempt economic progress has to be relegated to a secondary place, and that it has to be subordinated to noneconomic aims, such as full employment. Impoverishment is an evil; but not only does the impoverishment resulting from the armaments-race—not to mention a war—so far exceed any impoverishment due to social measures as to make the latter appear negligible; but impoverishment is also a far lesser evil than the complete collapse of freedom and liberties. To know this and to admit it is all the more important as all the social policies introduced by the western democracies as defense against the danger of totalitarian collapse have been vitiated by the pretense—made bona fide rather than fraudulently—that they would serve the cause of economic progress. Actually and necessarily they impede it. Not only have the wrong social measures therefore been taken, but the self-deception that these measures would prove economically beneficial lead to unnecessary economic damage which exceeded the economically bearable. Thereby the very liberties which should have been defended and strengthened have been jeopardized. The French "popular front" shows these dangers very clearly. But if it is recognized that necessary social policies must to some extent be economically harmful, they can be properly weighed as to their social benefits in relation to the economic sacrifices which they involve. And we would cease pretending that any such policy can be "good for business" or that a destruction of economic assets—which might socially be wholly beneficial and necessary—can become economically anything but harmful through the magic of "purchasing-power theories," "spending theories," and such like.

Even if we succeed fully in formulating such policies, they can at best prepare the ground. They cannot themselves create the new society. The new society must be accomplished by forces of a far more basic nature which can only be brought forth under pressure. The next decade will decide whether Europe can find such forces which would lead her out of the impasse into which the collapse of Economic Man has maneuvered her, or whether she has to grope her way through the darkness of totalitarian fascism before she finds a new, positive noneconomic concept of Free and Equal Man.

APPENDIX

ATHOLL, DUCHESS OF. *Katherine Marjory* (1874-1960), One of the first women to sit in the English Parliament, and an early and uncompromising opponent of appeasing Hitler.

BAADER, FRANZ XAVER VON. (1765-1841), German philosopher and mystic.

BALBO, ITALO. (1896-1940), Italian Fascist leader and aviator.

BARTH, KARL. (1886-1968), Swiss Protestant theologian, one of the leading thinkers of 20th-century Protestantism.

BERDIADIEV *(Berdyaev)*, NICHOLAS. (1874-1948), Russian religious philosopher and intellectual.

BERNANOS, GEORGES. (1888-1948), French novelist and polemicist.

BONALD, VICOMTE LOUIS GABRIEL AMBROISE DE. (1754-1840), French philosopher and publicist.

BOSCO, DON GIOVANNI. (1818-1888), Italian priest; founder, order of Salesian Fathers (1864), and of first social services for children in industrial slums.

BRUENING *(Brüning)*, HEINRICH. (1885-   ), German statesman; chancellor (1930-1932) and director of German foreign policy (1931).

CIANO, *in full* CIANO DI CORTELLAZZO, CONTE GALEAZZO. (1903-1944), Italian politician and Fascist leader; executed by Fascist authorities for high treason.

DÖLLINGER, JOHANN JOSEPH IGNAZ VON. (1799-1890), German theologian and historian, leader of the Old Catholics. Excommunicated in 1871 for refusing to accept doctrine of papal infallibility.

DONOSO CORTES, JUAN FRANCISCO MARIA DE LA SALUD. *Marques de Valdegamas* (1809-1853), Spanish orator, writer, statesman and diplomat.

DOUGLAS, CLIFFORD HUGH. (1879-1952), English social economist and engineer; author of economic theory of Social Credit.

FAULHABER, MICHAEL VON. (1869-1952), German churchman, cardinal of the Roman church; leading pacifist between the two world wars.

FISHER, IRVING. (1867-1947), American economist; noted for his studies in managed currency.

FRY, ELIZABETH (GURNEY). (1780-1845), English Quaker, philanthropist, and prison reformer.

FUNK, WALTHER. (1890-1960), German journalist and economist; minister of economics (1938); sentenced (1946) as war criminal to life imprisonment.

GÖRRES, JOSEPH VON. (1776-1848), German historian, journalist, and Romantic writer.

JUENGER *(Jünger)*, ERNST. (1895-   ), German writer whose view of war was incorporated in National Socialist ideology, but who later came to oppose Hitler.

KETTELER, BARON WILHELM EMMANUEL VON. (1811-1877), German Roman Catholic ecclesiastic leader; championed Christian Socialism and social and economic reforms.

KEYNES, JOHN MAYNARD, FIRST BARON OF TILTON. (1883-1946), English economist and monetary expert.

KINGSLEY, CHARLES. (1819-1875), English clergyman and novelist; identified with Christian Socialism.

LAMENNAIS, FÉLICITÉ ROBERT DE. (1782-1854), French philosopher, Roman Catholic Apologist, liberal; died excommunicate.

LEY, ROBERT. (1890-1945), German Nazi leader of anticommunism; committed suicide awaiting trial as a war criminal.

LITVINOFF, MAXIM MAXIMOVICH. (1876-1952), Russian Communist leader and statesman; said to have favored Soviet cooperation with Western powers.

MAISTRE, COMTE JOSEPH MARIE DE. (1753-1821), French ultraconservative statesman, and philosopher of Bourbon Restoration.

MATTEOTTI, GIACOMO. (1885-1924), Italian Socialist politician; murdered by Fascisti.

MAURIAC, FRANCOIS. (1885-   ), French writer and Nobel Prize winner.

MAURICE, FREDERICK DENISON. (1805-1872), English theologian and founder of Christian Socialism.

MICHELS, ROBERT. (1876-1936), Economist and sociologist; originally a prominent Socialist in his native Germany; later moved to Italy and became early ideologist of Fascism.

MILCH, ERHARD. (1892-   ), German air force commander, general, secretary of state in air ministry (1933).

MOELLER VAN DEN BRUCK, ARTHUR. (1876-1925), German Romantic conservative.

NIEMOELLER, MARTIN. (1892-   ), German anti-Nazi Protestant theologian.

OWEN, ROBERT. (1771-1858), British social reformer and Socialist; pioneer in the cooperative movement.

PAPEN, FRANZ VON. (1879-1969), German diplomat, soldier, statesman; chancellor (1932); vice chancellor in Hitler's cabinet (1933-1934); acquitted of major war crimes (1946).

PARETO, VILFREDO. (1848-1923), Economist and sociologist of Italian descent.

RADOWITZ, JOSEPH MARIA VON. (1797-1853), Prussian general and statesman.

RATHENAU, WALTER. (1867-1922), German industrialist, social theorist, and statesman; though a strong German nationalist, was assassinated by ultra-nationalist extremists while Foreign Minister—the first Jewish victim of Nazism.

ROSENBERG, ALFRED. (1893-1946), German National Socialist leader; supplied Hitler with spurious philosophical and scientific data for racist doctrine.

SCHACHT, HJALMAR. (1877-   ), German financier; minister of economy (1934) whose complicated, unorthodox program of currency exchange controls and barter trade abroad enabled Germany to secure materials for rearmament and extend its economic influence.

SCHLEGEL, FRIEDRICH VON. (1772-1829), German philosopher, critic, and writer; a founder of Romanticism.

SEIPEL, IGNAZ. (1876-1932), Austrian Roman Catholic prelate and head of Christian Socialist party; Austrian Prime Minister during most of 1920's.

SHAFTESBURY, LORD. *Anthony Ashley Cooper.* (1801-1885), 7th Earl of Shaftesbury, philanthropist, reformer; urged passage of first factory acts in England.

SOREL, GEORGES. (1847-1922), French journalist; leader in proclaiming philosophy of revolutionary syndicalism.

STAHL, FRIEDRICH JULIUS. (1802-1861), German lawyer, philosopher, and politician.

STARACE, ACHILLE. (1889-1945), Italian politician; secretary general of Fascist party (1932-1939); executed.

STRACHEY, JOHN. (1901-   ), British politician and writer of books on political and economic theory.

STRASSER, OTTO JOHAN MAXIMILIAN. (1897-   ), Early Nazi leader who later broke with Hitler.

STURZO, DON LUIGI. (1871-1959), Italian priest and political leader; opponent of Fascism.

CPSIA information can be obtained
at www.ICGtesting.com
Printed in the USA
LVHW080903201122
733639LV00015B/914